PROFESSIONAL DEVELOPMENT OF LOGISTICS ENGLISH TEACHERS

物流英语教师专业化发展

左　雁　吴尚义　编著

知识产权出版社
全国百佳图书出版单位

PROFESSIONAL DEVELOPMEN LOGISTICS ENGLISH TEACHER

责任编辑：国晓健　　　　　　**责任出版**：刘译文

图书在版编目（CIP）数据

物流英语教师专业化发展/左雁，吴尚义编著．—北京：知识产权出版社，2013.11

ISBN 978-7-5130-2420-4

Ⅰ．①物…　Ⅱ．①左…②吴…　Ⅲ．①物流—英语—教学参考资料　Ⅳ．①H31

中国版本图书馆CIP数据核字（2013）第269268号

Professional Development of Logistics English Teachers

物流英语教师专业化发展

WULIU YINGYU JIAOSHI ZHUANYEHUA FAZHAN

左　雁　吴尚义　编著

出版发行：知识产权出版社

社　址：北京市海淀区马甸南村1号	**邮　编**：100088
网　址：http：//www.ipph.cn	**邮　箱**：bjb@cnipr.com
发行电话：010-82000893	**传　真**：010-82000893
责编电话：010-82000860转8385	**责编邮箱**：guoxiaojian@cnipr.com
印　刷：知识产权出版社电子制印中心	**经　销**：新华书店及相关销售网点
开　本：787mm×1092mm　1/16	**印　张**：9.75
版　次：2014年1月第1版	**印　次**：2014年1月第1次印刷
字　数：288千字	**定　价**：29.00元

ISBN 978-7-5130-2420-4

内容简介

——帮助物流英语教师实现专业化发展

《物流英语教师专业化发展》试图梳理一下“教师专业化发展理论”与物流英语教师教育实践之间的关系，在训练活动中整合“专业化发展理论”，在课堂行为中显现“专业化发展”。意在帮助物流英语教师尽快适用新的理论，通过意识的改变、专业能力的训练，建构一个物流英语教学课堂中的新“我”，实现课堂面貌与课堂效果的变化，实现英语教育理论对专业英语课程改革的支持和支援功能，最终以自己为资源，完成物流英语教师的专业化发展。

如果你想了解物流英语教师专业化发展中的能力要求，这本书会以讨论的形式向你展开；如果你已经了解了物流英语教师专业化发展对能力的必然要求，这本书将与你讨论操作层面的教学问题，起到“跟进培训”的作用。

本书采用了比较灵活和轻松的体例：任务的凸显鲜明，是想产生一定的融入力和合作力；配插图，是想借助图画语言表达抽象思想，让教师在比较轻松的状态下学习；参与讨论，是想呼唤教师的参与意识，以便在教育经验基础上进行专业化发展的能力培训；理论之声，是想使教师得到思想的整理和理论的提升。这种体例，适合多种形式的物流英语教师培养和培训，也便于发展中教师的个人研读。

TABLE OF CONTENTS

Module One

Understanding of Logistics English Teachers

Discussion:

◇ What difficulties did logistics English teachers experience?

◇ What sort of logistics English teacher are you?

◇ What professional competences should logistics English teachers be equipped?

Section 1 Frustration of Logistics English Teachers

Problem and Reflection

Activity One: Fill in the activity card

1. Considering a logistics English teacher, what kinds of difficulties and problems will you think of?

2. What do you think of the problems and difficulties? What sorts of ways can you think of in solving the problems and overcoming the difficulties?

Activity Two: Reading

1. The following are talks from some English language teachers about their frustration. Do you agree with them? (Bailey, 2001)

A teacher can be compared to a battery. At the beginning of the school year, all the students are plugged in and drawing learning current. At the end of the school year, the battery is worn down and it must be recharged. And each time the battery is recharged it is more difficult to get it to hold its charge, and eventually it must be replaced. That is when complete burnout has taken place (Jim Y., a teacher, quoted in Maslach, 1982: 2)

Dick L., an elementary school teacher, is finding it increasingly uncomfortable to have a drink in the local bar after work. Once some other customers discover he is a teacher, they let him know the contempt they have for his profession—"You guys are doing a lousy job of teaching, and yet you have the nerve to demand bigger salaries. And you already get three months of vacation!" and so on, and so on (Maslach, 1982: 52).

After school, I work as a gymnastics coach. This gives me the opportunity to contact with students that is different from teaching, so it helps me see them in a different light and can offset some of the daily frustrations. Plus, it gives me a chance to exercise, work off tension, and keep in good physical condition. During the summer I get as far away from teaching as possible. I look forward to that summer job: lifeguard, house painter, salesman, or whatever. Sometimes, that job becomes a year-round vocation. Moonlighting is often a financial necessity because teachers' salaries are pretty inadequate. But, more importantly, it is an emotional survival technique (Roger E., a teacher, ibid., 88-89).

A teacher cannot function adequately for long without an informed shoulder to lean on, without an on-the-spot human wailing wall at which to gripe, to rage, to express fears and confess mistakes, to ask questions and wonder...Where the human wailing wall is carefully conceived and consistently offered, where the people provided are ... informed, sensitive, sympathetic, and understanding, the turnover among teachers, even under the most incredibly difficult conditions, is remarkably lowered (Long and Newman, 1961:5-26, as cited in Maslach, 1982:111).

2. Read the following interviews with two logistics English teachers. What do you think of their ideas?

Interview one

The first interview, with one logistics English teacher engaged in this field for more than five years, revealed the teacher's dissatisfaction towards the teaching situation in her class. The evaluation method there to the teachers does not fully reflect the teachers' teaching ability and teaching result. The existing administrative management to the teachers also irritated the teacher. Faced with no challenges from the present teaching tasks, she was fed up with the dull routine teaching. She didn't enjoy the teaching activities and was in the trouble of getting out of the distressed feelings.

Interview two

The second interview was conducted with a young logistics English teacher. It revealed a quite different response to the situation. The teacher had been working in the university for less than three years. She loved this career and she was very enthusiastic in doing everything connected with logistics English teaching, whereas, she was confused with a lot of teaching difficulties. The only way in solving the problem was getting advices from the experienced teacher. She also thought of the theory support ——getting teaching knowledge from the pedagogic works. However, she found the theory too difficult to be understood. She often asked the experienced teachers to explain the theory by showing simple teaching examples in logistics English teaching. She wants to learn everything, actually.

Activity Three: Discussion

1. As you were reading the above two accounts you probably thought about the differences and similarities befween the English language teachers and logistics English teachers. Considering the specific condition of logistics English teachers in China, especially your conditions as logistics English teachers, write notes under the following headings. You may add contents of them from your own experiences and your findings:

Frustration for the English language teachers	Frustration for the logistics English teachers

2. Read the following experiences written by Ur, penny (2000:330) about his way in struggling out of his frustration as being an English language teacher. Think of your ways of going out of frustration and discuss in pairs to get peer-support.

My recollections of my first year of teaching English as a foreign language are on the whole negative. There were, it is true, some positive aspects: an end-of-term play, for example, that children and parents enjoyed; the awareness that the children were progressing. But my main memories are of investing an enormous amount of work in preparing lessons and materials, much of which was in the event wasted; horrific discipline problems; feelings of disappointment and humiliation.

The outstanding event which helped me was at the end of my first year, when I went to the "homeroom" teacher of one of the classes I had been teaching and told him I thought I was unsuited to be a teacher and wished to leave. He told me to think less about my own feelings and to look at the students: to try to assess as objectively as I could what they had acquired from my teaching: mainly how much English they had learned, but also whether they had progressed in learning skills, and whether their motivation and attitude to the language had been enhanced. He said that if I honestly thought they had not learned, I should leave. I stayed.

3. Read the challenge of logistics and think of the requirement of the development to the logistics English teachers.

Although logistics has been a growing area of responsibility in many companies since the 1960s, it is fair to say that the profile of logistics managers in corporate America was not as high in most companies prior to 1980 as it is today. Logistics managers tended to be regarded as hard working individuals who played primarily a supporting role to marketing and manufacturing. However, the "back-to-basics" movement helped to change the profile level of logistics in the 1980s, particularly because a growing number of companies recognized the role that logistics can play at the margin in their strategic efforts to gain or regain a sustainable competitive edge? Efficient transportation systems support logistics practices such as "just-in-time" inventory and manufacturing; Vendor Managed Inventory (VMI); and Collaborative Planning; Fore-casting, and Replenishment (CPFR). Companies such as Pfizer and Wal-Mart have used these concepts to lower costs and gain significant market share.

The beginning of the 21st century actually saw a continuation of the evolution of logistics that began during the decades following World War II; however, since then, several variables have introduced new challenges: The Internet and e-business; Continued globalization; Business alliances; Rapidly changing technology.

Today, many of these firms have gained control of fulfillment operations through the use of private operations or third Party Logistics providers (3PLs). E-business over the Internet has quickly developed into a powerful medium for firms to reach customers through information, products, and services. This has put pressure on the logistics and transportation networks of shippers. Firms such as UPS and FedEx Ground have seen an explosion of small package deliveries to both business and residential addresses. Shipment sizes have decreased and frequency of shipments have increased. Real – time inventory tracking has allowed companies in the supply chain to eliminate inventories. Reliable transportation networks have also allowed firms to eliminate unnecessary safety stock inventories. With all of these challenges, the use of the Internet for e–business is still in the developmental stage.

The globalization of business has had a tremendous impact on the way companies operate today. The scope of globalization runs the gamut from foreign sourcing in the procurement area and/or selective sales in other countries to multifaceted international distribution, manufacturing, and marketing strategies that encompass international production sites, multiple staging of inventory, counter trading in the sale of products, and so on. Whatever the situation, the cost of logistics as a percentage of total cost is greater for international ventures, and the complexity of logistics operations usually increases at a geometric rate in the international arena. If procurement is included, logistics is the single–most important factor for successful international ventures. Transportation, in particular, has been affected because of the distances involves both inbound to manufacturing from foreign sourcing and outbound for additional manufacturing or delivery to customers. Transportation might account for as much as 50 percent of the total logistics costs.

The 1990s saw a dramatic growth in the use of 3PLs for basic transportation and distribution processes. This growth continues in the 2000s with 3PLs expanding their services to include inventory management, order management, and inventory ownership. These relationships allow 3PLs to gain a larger "share of wallet" of their clients business. This is one example of the change in the nature of business alliances that are being developed in industry. The beginning of this decade has seen Amazon. com performing fulfillment for Toys "Я" Us. com, WalMart. com out–sourcing their Internet fulfillment operations, US Airways and United Airlines joining forces to share flights, fares, and frequent traveler programs, and food manufacturers sharing capacity in transportation vehicles for customer deliveries. The 2000s have brought a new type of alliance among companies, which are some times competitors. These alliances focus on eliminating duplication of assets and processes so that both parties can benefit. The remainder of the 2000s will more than likely see more innovative types of business alliances.

Another factor is rapidly changing technology and, in particular, changes in computer hardware and software. The significant price reductions for powerful computer equipment have helped bring about better inventory control, better equipment scheduling, more efficient rating of transportation movements, and so on. Technological changes in communications, such as satellite global positioning systems to maintain contact with motor carrier fleets, have helped to improve service quality to the extent that motor carrier companies now are able to meet narrowly defined timewindows for pickups and deliveries. The continued development of Radio Frequency Identification (RFID) is allowing companies to track freight to the individual package level. The interface between communication technology and computers is another area that has tremendous potential for logistics. These changes are just the tip of the iceberg, many other developments could be included in this area, such as bar coding and robotics.

All of these challenges have provided opportunities for logistics and transportation processes to add value to product movement throughout the globe. They have also given the logistics and transportation processes more responsibility for the management of information and cash flows throughout the supply chain.

Voice from the Theory

Understanding the role of EFL teachers. (Transcribed from a speech at the 1st International Annual Conference of TEFL-CHINA, 2002)

Teacher's consciousness of their role is essential in their professional development. The terms that denote a teacher's role are indeed many. Different methods have different assumption about what role the teacher plays in the classroom. The term "role" has been defined in two different ways:

The first one: a role can be defined generally as "a part people play in the performance of social life" (Widdowson, R. G).

"A role is a set of norms and expectations applied to the incumbency of a particular position"——(sociologist)

The focal type of teacher role is occupational and identifying. It is a position with a certain responsibilities and expectations. In the classroom, a teacher in this type of clothes is in contrast with the student and the pupil, both of which are also identifying but not in contrast with the word learner.

The later type of role is manifest to the learner. It is transactional and incidental. The transactional part of role is more sophisticated as the teaching and learning process goes along, the teacher may serve as a model in using the type of language, an organizer in conducting activities, a counselor in diagnosing the learners' problems and giving good advise, and participant-observer of the teaching and learning process, etc.

This division of teacher's roles is useful in understanding the authority of the teacher in the classroom. Widdowson points out that the identifying role is authoritarian, while the transactional role is authoritative. In Chinese the identifying role is "权力性", the transitional role is "业务性".

Widdowson makes a very important point here.

How we view the exercise of authority in action depend more on our attitude for education and the society it serves. And perhaps this is indeed necessary for the maintenance of an open society. If that is made, this is quite a different issue from exercise of authority in transaction or no matter how we view pedagogy, no matter how much initiative we allow for the learner, the teacher must surely retain an undiminished authority. Increase in learner-centered activity and corroborative work in classroom, does not mean that the teacher becomes less authoritative. He/she still has to comply with the required convenient conditions for learning, still has to monitor and guide the pupils.

No educational reforms or educational innovations will diminish the authority of the transactional type of law. Pedagogical observations show that the more innovative the teacher is, the more transactional roles he /she plays, the more authoritative he/she is before the learners.

In the current education reform in China, it is necessary to distinguish between two types of roles of the teacher and to keep in mind Widdowson's advise, specifically, while adopting learner-centered task based on teaching and learning. We shall need to retain the authority of the teacher.

The continuing development of teachers is therefore a key link in promoting any educational reform.

三 Understanding the definitions of logistics

What is logistics in the sense that it is understood today? There are a number of definitions of what is understood by the word logistics and, in some senses, the use of the word is simple, while in others it is more complex. The following definitions will help you understand the term:

① Logistics (business definition): Logistics is defined as a business - planning framework for the management of material, service, information and capital flows. It includes the increasingly complex information, communication and control systems required in today's business environment.

——(Logistics Partners Oy, Helsinki, FI,1996)

② Logistics (military definition): The science of planning and carrying out the movement and maintenance of forces— "those aspects of military operations that deal with the design and development, acquisition, storage, movement, distribution, maintenance, evacuation and disposition of material; movement and hospitalization of personnel; acquisition of construction, maintenance, operation and disposition of facilities; and acquisition of furnishing of services".

—— (JCS Pub 1-02 excerpt)

③Logistics: The procurement, maintenance, distribution, and replacement of personnel and material.

—— (Webster's Dictionary)

④Logistics: The art of maintaining control over worldwide supply chains by a combination of transport, warehousing skills, distribution management and information technology.

—— (Benson, R. and Whitehead, T. S. Transport and Logistics)

⑤Logistics: The process of strategically managing the movement and storage of raw materials, component parts and finished goods throughout the business from suppliers to final delivery to customers.

——(Christopher, M. Logistics: the Strategic Issues)

⑥Logistics: 1. The branch of military operations that deals with the procurement, distribution, maintenance, and replacement of material and personnel. 2. The management of the details of an operation.

——(American Heritage Dictionary)

⑦ Logistics: The process of planning, implementing, and controlling the efficient, effective flow and storage of goods, services, and related information from point of origin to point of consumption for the purpose of conforming to customer requirements. Note that this definition includes inbound, outbound, internal, and external movements, and return of materials for environmental purposes.

——(Reference: Council of Logistics Management)

⑧Logistics: The process of planning, implementing, and controlling the efficient, cost effective flow and storage of raw materials, in-process inventory, finished goods and related information from point of origin to point of consumption for the purpose of meeting customer requirements.

——(References: Canadian Association of Logistics Management)

From these definitions logistics can be briefly described like this: logistics means having the right thing, in the right place, at the right time. The underlying concept might be defined as follows:

Logistics is the process of planning, implementing, and controlling the efficient, effective flow and storage of raw materials, in-process inventory, finished goods, services, and related information from point of origin to point of consumption (including inbound, outbound, internal, and external movements) for the purpose of confirming to customer requirements. Implied in the definition is that the logistics process provides a systems framework for decision making that integrates transportation, inventory levels, warehousing space, materials-handling systems, packaging, and other related activities that encompass appropriate trade-offs involving cost and service.

貳 Understanding the definition of supply chain

A supply chain is a complex logistics system in which raw materials are converted into finished products and then distributed to the final users (consumers or companies). It includes suppliers, manufacturers, warehouses, DCs and retail outlets.

It is characteristic of a supply chain that each node on the chain depends on the nodes before it. For example, raw materials cannot be processed into finished goods unless they are transported to the factory at first. This means that the failure of one chain will result in the failure of the whole chain. No one element of the chain is more or less important than all the others.

Not all supply chains remain the same. Different products or sectors can have a different supply chain.

Section 2　Picture Yourself as a Logistics English Teacher

Problem and Reflection

Activity One: Finding words

1. Use as many adjectives as you can think of to describe a good logistics English teacher, list them.

A goodlogistics English teacher is:

2. Use as many adjectives as you can think of to describe an inadequate logistics English teacher, list them.

An inadequate logistics English teacher is:

3. Discuss with your peers about the answers to the above two activities. Find the words that best describe you as a logistics English teacher.

As a logistics English teacher, I am ___________.

Activity Two: Reading

1. Pre-reading task: discussion

Discuss with your peers about the topic "What do you think of your logistics English teaching?" The procedure is as follows:

a) Each person writes 20 sentences. Each sentence should have the content of logistics English teaching and the subject is "I" or "My logistics English teaching".

b) Change your sentences with your partner.

c) Discuss about the meaning of these sentences and share the views on logistics English teaching.

Read the following article transcribed from a speech at the 1st International Annual Conference of TEFL-CHINA, 2002.

Promoting Professional Development of EFL teachers

This is an on-going process of becoming better in performing his/her roles. How well the teacher performs his role depends on the training and retraining that he receives. The past teacher training programmes are generally based on knowledge-skill models and this has been shown as being inadequate in the new era.

Courses that can develop trainee's awareness of the multifaceted nature of language and the multidisciplinary nature of language teaching should be added into the teacher training programmes. It is necessary for trainees to learn pedagogy, grammar, linguistics, and applied linguistics.

In addition to holding pre-service training programmes, there are also guidelines for the in-service professional development of teachers. Teachers become mature in the process of teaching.

How can our EFL teachers develop competency to become true professionals?

A 3-R Approach is proposed here, based on various studies, to guide young EFL teachers.

a) Summarize ones own teaching and to locate problems. In the past 20years or so, many western educators have reconsidered perfecting the effectiveness of practical personality in education. Indeed a rational personality has a strong influence on the educational profession.

Teaching is not simply a process of delivering knowledge by mechanically applying certain techniques. The teacher needs to concentrate, reflect upon his teaching, realizing the complexity of the profession, and its various variables. Analyzing means, to understand the direction of the variables, to find problems, and to find more options in classroom handling.

b) Ready to communicate with specialists of contributing disciplines. How to teach is closely related to what to teach, and how learning takes place. Methodology is a force that helps the teacher to a certain extent. Therefore a true professional must consult with others in the same field and specialists of relevant disciplines. Teaching Language requires an understanding of the nature of the language, and the process of language learning, and the understanding of the essence of education. EFL teachers need to read publications in linguistics, applied linguistics, psycholinguistics and pedagogy. Language teachers need to communicate with linguists. The purpose is not to get direct answers to the questions that the teacher is faced with but insights into the nature of language. Linguistics contributes to language teaching by providing linguistic descriptions for designing syllabuses or developing materials.

The problematic chart proposed by Holiday (1978) has expanded the scope of language study to four overlapping points.

i) Language as a system, that is, foreign and private system, grammar and vocabulary.

ii) Language is knowledge and thought.

iii) Knowledge as behavior active in the social context.

iv) Language as an art or as a particular way of representing and describing reality.

The multifaceted nature of language proves that language teaching is complicated. Teaching and learning activities, decides what is actually learnt. Teachers must also decide what to teach.

Therefore, professional teachers should keep abreast with innovations in syllabus designing and text-book writing.

c) Researching for innovation.

Many applied linguists have pointed out that language teachers should not be merely consumers of theory they can also be producers theory. Research is nothing mysterious, it starts with the classroom. Once a teacher has found a classroom, which is suitable for research, he/she has already has a starting point for a project. Formulating hypothesis and verifying it through experimental classes a teacher may find his/her own solution.

In China today, the society lays great emphasis on creativity and innovation.

Teaching is inherently creative and innovative. Teachers as professionals are not just practitioners but must innovate.

To end this paper, I would like to contradict a Chinese saying "Teachers are burning candles". This metaphor has negative tone in that teaching is seen as an impoverished situation rather than an enriching process. No teacher became less knowledgeable because of teaching. In fact all teachers become more mature and more knowledgeable through teaching. If the value of education lies in helping the students to learn what to be, what to do and how to learn, then teachers must consciously and unconsciously develop their competency to become true professionals.

Post-reading task:

After reading it, think of the question "How can one become a good logistics English teacher?" and find the answer in pairs. (The hint is hidden somewhere in this module)

Activity Three: Discussion

1. Free discussion

Facing the challenge of the new era, what aspects should the logistics English teachers change, or what are the necessary competences the present logistics English teachers should have? Discuss in a group to get the opinions.

2. Reading for appreciation (Cited from Carter & Nunan, 2001)

English for Specific Purposes (ESP) has for about 30 years been a separate branch of English Language Teaching. It has developed its own approaches, materials and methodology and is generally seen as a very active, even "feisty" moment that has had considerable influence over the more general activities of TESOL and applied linguistics.

As with most branches of TESOL and applied linguistics, ESP is often divided up into various categories with mysterious acronyms. It is usually classified into two main categories: English for Academic Purposes (EAP) and English for Occupational Purposes (EOP). EAP largely speaks for itself: it relates to the English needed in an educational context, usually at a university or similar institution, and possibly also at school level. EOP is more complicated: it relates to professional purposes, e. g. those of working doctors, engineers or business people. The biggest branch of EOP is business English, the teaching of which can range from teaching general business-related vocabulary to the teaching of specific skills important in business, e. g. negotiation and meeting skills.

The key defining feature of ESP is that its teaching and materials are founded on the results of needs analysis. The first question when starting preparation for teaching an ESP course is almost always: What do students need to do with English? Which of the skills do they need to master and how well? Which genres do they need to master, either for comprehension or production purposes? Various commentators have remarked that needs analysis is not exclusive to ESP and that much general TESOL—especially when following the communicative approach—is based on needs analysis. However, in ESP one can be more precise about learners' needs, their needs are defined by a learning or occupational situation in which English plays a key role. Specific needs can be identified by examining that situation and the texts in detail; in contrast, for students not immediately using English, or about to use it, needs are much more general.

The ESP teacher needs to bear in mind and exploit if possible this specific subject knowledge, which leads to classroom interaction and teaching methodology that can be quite different from that of general English, however, in some situation, e. g. pre-study or pre - work courses where learners have not started their academic of professional activity and therefore have less subject knowledge, teaching methodology will be similar to that of general English. The use of a distinctive methodology is therefore a variable characteristic of ESP.

We therefore return to the question of the defining features of ESP. Looking closely a"specific purpose", ESP materials will always draw on the topics and activities of that specific purpose, in many cases exploiting the methodology of the subject area or the profession. For example, an English course for engineers will use engineering situations to present relevant language and discourse; problem-solving activities will probably also be used, since they draw on skills and abilities possessed by the students. Similarly, a business English course will use case studies as these are widely used in business training. It must not, however, be forgotten that ESP is concerned with teaching language, discourse and relevant communication skills; it exploits topics and the underlying methodology of the target discipline or profession to present language, discourse and skills.

I thus see the absolute characteristics of ESP as follows:

— ESP is designed to meet the specific needs of the learner.

— ESP makes use of the underlying methodology and activities of the discipline it serves.

— ESP is centered on the language skills, discourse and genres appropriate to these activities.

The hint to post-reading discussion:

How can one become a good logistics English teacher?

- The most important and difficult part of the task is developing professional competence.
- Professional competence is more complicated and difficult than some other skills, such as driving or speaking a foreign language.
- Wallace's Reflective Model" (as a reference):
  - Stage 1: language training
  - Stage 2: learning, practice and reflection
  - Stage 3: the goal (professional competence)

Bibliography

Bailey, K. M., Curtis, A., & Nunan, D. 2001. *Pursuing professional development: the self as source*[M]. Thomson Learning.

Johnson, K., Johnson, H. 1999. *Encyclopedic Dictionary of Applied Linguistics: A Handbook for Language Teaching* [M]. Blackwell Publishers Ltd.

Richards, J. C., Platt, J., Platt, H. (Ed.). 1998. *Longman Dictionary of Language Teaching & Applied Linguistics* [M]. Beijing: Addison Longman China Limited.

Ur, P.. 2000. *A course in Language Teaching: Practice and Theory* [M]. Cambridge: Cambridge University press.

Wallace, M. J. 1992. *Training Foreign Language Teachers* [M]. Cambridge: Cambridge University Press.

Module Two

Self-reflection Competence of Logistics English Teachers

Discussion:

◇ How do you understand *reflection*?

◇ How many forms of *reflection* are there?

◇ How do you design *the reflective teaching*?

Section 1 Understanding Reflection

Problem and Reflection

Activity One: Lead-in knowledge

Imagine that it is the end of a teaching day and you've just finished a class that didn't go well/ that was very successful. As you leave the school and head home, you think about this class. What runs through your mind? How do you reflect on what happened? Which do you think you may spend more time on it, a class that didn't go well or a successful class?

A class that didn't go well	A successful class
Reflect on: 1. 2. 3. 4. 5.	Reflect on: 1. 2. 3. 4. 5.

Activity Two: Reading

Read the following dialogues about reflection, may you understand the definition of "reflective teaching" better? (Adapted from Bailey, K. M., 2004:34-36)

Kathi: So Mark, congratulations on your new teaching job. Who are your students and what are you teaching?

Mark: Thanks, Kathi! I am very excited. I have six ESL students, four from Japan, one from Vietnam, and one from Korea. It's challenging because they all have varying degrees of experience, from an extreme beginning level to high intermediate. They are fun to teach, though—outgoing, friendly, and extremely willing to learn. Right now, I'm teaching several classes, which is hard because I'm still going to school myself. I'm teaching two reading classes, a TOEFL grammar class, an autobiographical writing class, and a community experience class where I take them on field trips. For instance, I took them to the Monterey Police Department this morning, and they got to try on handcuffs and bulletproof vests. They loved it, and so did I!

Kathi: Have you had any teaching experience in the past?

Mark: I have very little experience in teaching. Last semester I volunteered in a conversation class for a month. I started teaching regularly a month ago, and I have really enjoyed it. It's a challenge, but I feel like it has taught me so much about what works and what doesn't work in a real classroom setting. Experience is definitely the key.

Kathi: I understand you decided you wanted to add an element of reflective practice to your teaching. What is exactly that you are doing?

Mark: Well, I thought it would be good to keep a journal of my teaching from the outset of my professional development. What better way to improve myself than to start thinking about my teaching practice at the beginning, right? So I decided to keep a journal in combination with opening up my class to observers on a regular basis. That way, I can get a good idea of what others see in me as a novice teacher and what it is I see in myself. Comparing these two kinds of information, I feel, will propel me into becoming a better teacher much faster than if I just went to class every day and didn't think about what I was doing.

Kathi: What have you learned so far by doing this?

Mark: So far I have found that I am concerned with reaching (or not reaching) my lowest level student. Looking back through my journal, I notice that I mention him often. I feel like I am leaving him behind so that the rest of the class isn't bored. I'm trying to find ways to keep everyone involved. I think I am going to do pair work with him personally, and let the others work with each other instead, because they seem frustrated when they're placed in a group with him.

Some observers have told me that I look very organized and experienced, which is hilarious to me since those are the two things I worry about most: being unprepared and appearing like a novice. It is so helpful to get outside feedback because, as with most aspects in life, teaching included, we are our own worst critic and can dwell on parts of ourselves that are already developed. Because of this feedback, I feel more confident in my abilities, and more willing to focus on other areas of my teaching, like board work, which I might have not even thought about when I was preoccupied with my preparation.

Kathi: How often do you make entries in your journal?

Mark: I try to write my journal after every class session, but there isn't always time. If I can't write immediately after class, I try to do so within the next few days so the class period is still fresh in my mind. I usually write for at least half an hour. I look forward to getting written feedback from my observers so I can start comparing that to what I have written. I have enjoyed the oral feedback, but I am excited to see what the observers have to say when they have had a chance to reflect a bit more.

Post-reading task:

Make a list of the contents that logistics English teacher should reflect on the teaching activities. The first two aspects have been given.

Logistics English teacher should reflect on
1. The teaching process
2. The teaching achievement
3.
4.
5.

Activity Three: Discussion

Look at the following model (Wallace, 1998:12) carefully, discuss the meaning and explain the model in your own words.

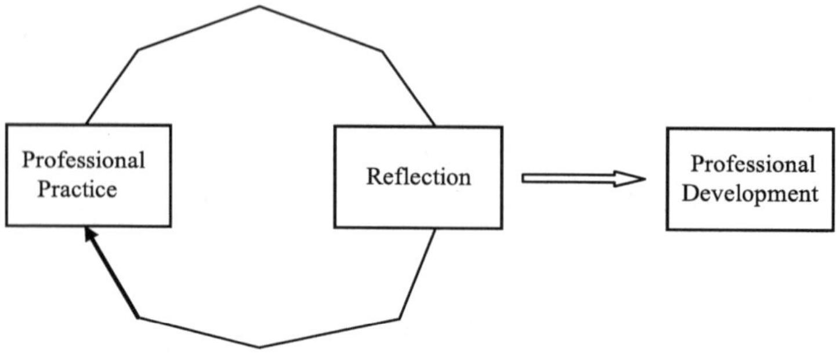

"REFLECTIVE CYCLE"

Voice from the Theory

- The literature on the use of reflection in teacher development has drawn largely on Dewey's distinction between reflective and routine action. Reflective action is that which engages the "active, persistent and careful consideration of any belief or supposed form of knowledge in the light of the grounds that support it and the consequences to which it leads" (Dewey, 1933). Routine action is that which is guided primarily by tradition, external authority and circumstance (Dewey, 1933; cited in Zeichner and Liston, 1987). Within the teacher development literature it is assumed that reflective teachers can be developed through teacher education programmes that encourage open-mindedness and responsibility, and that develop skills in observation and analysis.
- Cruickshank (1981:4) defines reflective teaching as the teacher's thinking about what happens in classroom lessons, and thinking about alternative means of achieving goals or aims; he sees it as a means to provide students with "an opportunity to consider the teaching event thoughtfully, and analytically and objectively".
- Zeichner and Liston (1985) propose a quite different perspective. They argue, "A reflective teacher is defined as one who assesses the origins, purposes and consequences of his or her work at all levels".

Section 2 Forms of Reflection

Problem and Reflection

Activity One: lead-in knowledge (Arnold, 2000:110)

In the first part of the twentieth century, John Dewey recognized the fact that most people and most teachers do not know how to use reflection as a tool for changing their classrooms, their lives and our societies. Thus, he devoted a major part of his life work to establishing what he knew reflection tobe (How We Think, 1933), and in creating teacher education programs which developed teachers who could not only look back at what had happened in their classrooms in detail, but could also analyze why certain events took place and what next steps needed to be taken. Deway's work and more recently that of Donald Schon (1983, 1987, 1991) have presented the purposeful process of reflection as having the following sequence:

- *think* back
- try to *remember* as much detail of the events as possible
- *investigate* reasons for the events
- *re-fram* eevents in light of several theoretical frameworks
- *generate* multiple understandings
- *decide* on what needs to be done next in relation to the analysis of what has already happened

Think of your way in reflecting on your teaching. Do you follow the same sequence with the above or have some differences? Where are the differences? Check it by writing down your sequences of reflection on your teaching.

My sequences in reflection on my teaching:
–
–
–
–
–

Activity Two: Reading (Arnold, 2000:119)

The following text is an example of microscopic reflection. The text is an excerpt from a paper the teacher wrote during her training practicum after looking at a videotape of her class.

Review of vocabulary: This section (of the lesson) was intended as a quick review, but ongoing student feedback told me that half of them didn't really know the words. The class was dragging and I wanted to see if they all understood the vocabulary. Having individual students come up (to the blackboard) to point and others to say it got the class more involved. Also, I could confirm if their lack of oral response was because they didn't know it. At this point the class energy picked up——they were helping each other, more actively participating individually and as a whole group in reading and pronouncing. Students in front were listening and pointing.

Sometimes I find it hard to read the "no response" mode, sometimes it's because they are just plain tired, other times bored, other times they don't know the material. This review section was not very challenging to the more advanced students, (and) I felt although it was quite teacher-directed, I tried to rely more on the students, make it more student-directed by having them come up and point and other students ask/tell. I was also trying to get the more advanced students to use more difficult words to challenge them while the slower ones were up front.

On the tape I see how much I interfered and repeated, when I thought I was giving them a chance to do more of the work. Maybe rather than approach (the class) from a traditional teacher to students way, (I could) give them more opportunities to work with the language among themselves.

Post-reading task:

The following list the regular used tools for reflection (Stanley, 1999). Tick the ones you have ever used and fill in the blanks the advantages and disadvantages of each.

Tools for reflection	Advantages	Disadvantages	The item you have ever used
The reflective teaching journal			
A cassette or video recording of a lesson			
A dialogue with another person			

Activity Three: Discussion

Reflecting time: Different teachers have the different time for reflection. Choose from the following choices your favorite time in reflection and state the reasons:

- immediately after a lesson
- at the end of a teaching day
- on the following morning before teaching once again
- other time

Reasons:

Tips: (Personal reflection)
If you have not done it before, try writing down your thoughts about lessons you have taught or will teach, say twice or three times a week. This can be in a rough scrawl—It does not matter if it is illegible to anyone else! You can use a separate notebook (journal), or make brief notes at the bottom of your lesson plans. After a while, reread your notes. Do you find them interesting? Useful as reminders? Thought-provoking? (Ur, 2000:319)

Voice from the Theory

- REFLECTIVE TEACHING[1] (Richards, 1998:390) —— An activity sometimes used in teacher preparation programmes which aims to provide student teachers with a controlled teaching experience and a chance to consider the nature of teaching thoughtfully and objectively.
- REFLECTIVE TEACHING[2] (Richards, 1998: 391) ——An approach to teaching and to teacher education which is based on the assumption that teachers can improve their understanding of teaching and the quality of their own teaching by reflecting critically on their teaching experiences. In teacher education programmes, activities which seek to develop a reflective approach to teaching aim to develop the skills of considering the teaching process thoughtfully, analytically and objectively, as a way of improving classroom practices.

Section 3 The Whole Designing of "Reflective Teaching" for Logistics English Teachers

Problem and Reflection

Activity One:

"The reflective teaching" is a spiral process which involves the procedures of planning, executing, observing & analyzing and reflecting, etc. NCNiff described these procedures as the following 5 specific processes:

1. Teachers discover the existing problems in teaching.
2. Teachers put forward the corresponding solving methods.
3. Teachers plan and execute the solving methods.
4. Teachers collect and analyze the data to evaluate the result.
5. Teachers discover new problems on the basis of analyzing and evaluation.

Study these processes carefully, then design your own "reflective teaching" with the aim of solving your own problems in the logistics English teaching. (The following reading may be a help to you.)

Problem:
Solving methods: 1. 2. 3. 4.
Teaching activities:
Evaluation:

Activity Two: Reading

The following is an example of "reflective teaching" being done in Nanjing, China. Read it to find some clues for your own reflective teaching.

ONE CASE STUDY

(The reflective teaching in English oral class)

Problem:

During the teaching of oral English, the teacher found that most of the students kept too silent and reluctant to open their mouths. The students showed little interest in the topics discussed in class. The teacher found it hard to change the situation.

Solutions:

By analyzing, the teacher decided to take the following steps:

a. After discussing in a group, the teachers decided some topics which were close to the students' life (e. g. My favorite job). These topics were assigned to the students for preparation.

b. Encourage the students to have a conversation with the parents on these topics to get more information and emotional input.

c. The teachers designed the following figure to attract the students for more thought and expressing.

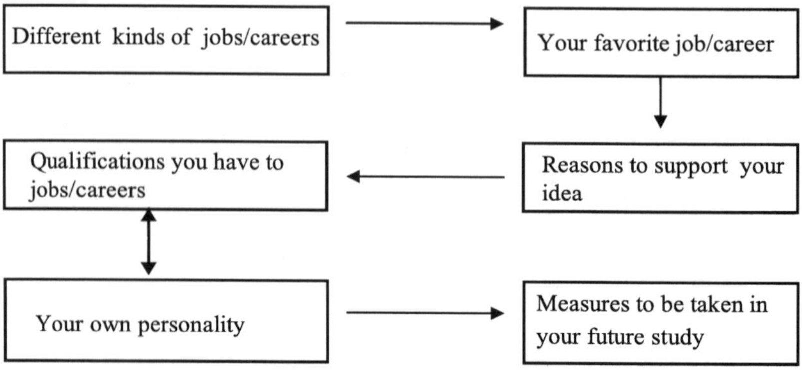

Teaching activities:

a. On class, the students are encouraged to change ideas in pairs. The aim of it is to communicate and gather information.

b. After discussing in groups, the teacher selects purposefully the shy students and weak expressers to report.

c. The teacher comments on the report and encourages the oral behaviors.

Evaluation:

This kind of teaching activates the students' interest in large sense. By giving more chances for the shy and weak students in spoken English, their confidence was built and their active participation also improved the teaching efficiency in class. More advantages will be discussed in detail...

(An article transcribed from a speech at the twelfth academic conference of the national foreign language teaching & research association, China education society, 2003)

Bibliography

Cruickshank, D. R., and Applegate, J. H. 1981. Reflective teaching as a strategy for teacher growth [J]. *Educational Leadership* 38:553-4.

Zeichner, K. M., and Liston D. P. 1985. *An inquiry-oriented approach to student teaching* [R]. Paper presented at the Practicum Conference. Geelong, Australia.

Arnold, J. 2000. *Affect in Language Learning* [M]. Cambridge: Cambridge University Press.

Ur, P. 1996. *A course in Language Teaching: Practice and Theory* [M]. Cambridge: Cambridge University Press.

Johnson, K., & Johnson, H. 1998. *Encyclopedic Dictionary of Applied Linguistics: a Handbook for Language Teaching* [M]. Blackwell Publishers Ltd.

Richards, J. C., Platt, J., & Platt, H. 1998. *Longman Dictionary of Language Teaching & Applied Linguistics* [M]. Addison Longman China Limited.

Module Three

Professional Competence of Logistics

Discussion:

◇ What are the features of logistics English?

◇ What kind of logistics professional knowledge are you equipped with?

◇ What are the components of a logistics system?

Section 1 Understanding Logistics English

Problem and Reflection

Activity One: List the specific features of logistics English

1.
2.
3.
4.
5.

Activity Two: Reading

A: Read the following dialogue to find out "What is logistics?".

What do we do?

Janet, a college graduate majoring in logistics, has just been recruited in a logistics firm, and she is trying to learn more about logistics from Martin, her manager.

Janet: I find practical logistics quite different from what we learn in books.

Martin: That's true. There is always a gap between theory and practice. And... (smile) you're here to fill the gap.

Janet: I'm eager to learn in my new job.

Martin: Good. Interest is the best teacher.

Janet: To begin with, how do you define logistics in the practical way?

Martin: Well, you may define logistics in a variety of ways. However, in simple terms, I'd say logistics is the flow and storage of goods from the point to origin to the point of consumption.

Janet: What is the core of logistics operation?

Martin: Logistics operation is mainly involved with movement of goods.

Janet: In routine logistics operation, what parties are involved?

Martin: Generally speaking, we have the suppliers, manufacturers, distributors, wholesalers, retailers, customers and so on.

Janet: Then do we also get into contact with government functions?

Martin: Occasionally. It is sometimes inevitable to seek government's assistance where necessary.

Janet: What is the scope of business that logistics covers?

Martin: Logistics covers a wide range of activities such as purchasing, transport, warehousing, outsourcing, inventory management, packaging, JIT delivery, information, customer service and so on.

Janet: Which specific activities is our company engaged in?

Martin: Our company specializes in JITD – just in time distribution – to our customers. We also provide warehousing and packaging services.

Janet: I do feel I have a lot to learn.

Martin: Take it easy. I'll be with you.

B: Read the following dialogue to find out "What is a supply chain?"

What is a supply chain?

Janet: Please tell me what is a supply chain.

Martin: A supply chain is a complex logistics system in which raw materials are converted into finished products and then distributed to the final users.

Janet: What parties are involved in the supply chain?

Martin: A typical supply chain normally includes suppliers, manufacturers, warehouses, DCs and retail outlets.

Janet: Then what is the difference between logistics and the supply chain?

Martin: That's a big question. But first logistics is part of the supply chain process, and...

Janet: ...and it focuses on the flow and storage of goods.

Martin: Exactly. Whereas a supply chain focuses on the whole distribution process in which goods travel from suppliers through distributors to end users.

Janet: What is SCM—supply chain management?

Martin: SCM is to integrate, coordinate and control the flow of material, information and finances in supply chains.

Janet: I hear there are two typical supply chain categories: the pull and push systems.

Martin: You are right.

Janet: What does NTO mean?

Martin: MTO stands for make to order.

Janet: How does it work?

Martin: MTO means the manufacturer does not begin to make the product until or unless after it receives the order from the customer.

Janet: How about inventory?

Martin: MTO is an order - driven supply chain model and in this model the manufacturer does not hold inventories in usual cases.

Janet: Can I say MTS—make to stock—is the opposite of MTO?

Martin: You may well say so.

Janet: How does MTS work?

Martin: Production planners forecast and estimate the effective demand and inventories are held in warehouses and at the retailers.

Janet: That means MTS is a forecast-driven supply chain model.

Martin: Exactly.

Activity Three:

The wide use of abbreviations is one feature of logistics English. As a logistics English teacher, the mastery of the kind of abbreviation is a necessary. Read the following and find out the ones that you are not familiar with. (The answer is at the end of this module)

3PL	AEO	API
4PL	AMS	ARENA
AAR	ALC	AS/RS
4SC	APEC	AWB
ACI	APS	ASEAN

API
B2B
B2C
BAF
B/B
BCO
BIFA
BIMCO
B/L
BPM
BPO
CAF
CAGR
CAP
CBM
C&F
CC
CCPIT
CDC
CKD
CDMA
CEP
CEPA
CFM
CFR
COFC
CFS
CGI
CKD
CIF

CILT
CIM
CIM
CIP
CLP
C/O
C. O. C.
C. O. D.
COFC
CPFR
CPG
CPT
CSC
CSI
CTN
CY
C&F
D/A
DAF
DCC
DDC
DDP
DDU
DES
DEQ
D. G.
DIP
DIY
D/O
D/P

DPP
DPWN
DRP
D/R
EAN
ECR
EDC
EDIFACT
EBIDS
EDI
EEC
EEZ
ELA
EMEA
EPC
ERM
ERP
ETD
ETA
ETO
EXW
FAA
FAF
FAO
FAK
FAS
FB/L
FCL
FCR
FDI

FEFC
FEU
FGP
F. I.
FIATA
FIFO
F. I. O.
FLOST
FMC
FMCG
FOB
FOC
F. O.
F. O. R.
F. O. T.
F/R
FRC
FTAA
FTP
FTZ
FTL
GATT
GDP
GRI
GSA
GSC
GWT
HAFFA
HAWB
H/H
LASH
LAN
L/C
LCL
L/C
L. I.
LILO
L. I. O.
L. O. A.
Lo-Lo ship
Lot-for-Lot
LLP
LNG
LPG
LSP
LT
LTL
IADA
I. A. Rates
IATA
IBC
ICAO
ICC
ICD
ICP
ICT
ICAR
IDA
IGD
IMDG
IMF
IMO
Incoterm
IP
IP
IPI
IPPC
IRA
ISDN
ISO
ISP
ISPS
I. A. Rates
M&A
MAI
MAWB
MERCOSUR
MLB
MLO
MNC
MOFTEC
MRP
MPL
M/S
MSDS
MTO
N/A
NAFTA
NAP
NFC

N. O. E.
N. O. S.
NVOCC
OCP
OECD
OEM
O/H
ORC
O/S
O/T
OTC
OTIF
O/W
PBOC
PCC
PCS
PEQ
P&I Club
PQ Order
POD
POL
POP
PPP
PRD
PSS
RCH
RF
RFI
RFP
RFQ
RFRC
Ro-Ro ship
ROCE
ROI
RRS
R/T
SAD
SAN
S/C
SCOR
SDR
SET
SKU
SLA
SME
S/O
S. O. C.
SQL
S/S
SSL
S. T. C.
S/O S/I
TACA
TCP
TEU
T. H. C.
TMS
TOFC
TQC
TQM
T. R. S.
TSA
T/S
TSR
TT
T/T
TUPE
TVC
TWRA
UCP500
USDA
ULCC
UNCTAD
V. A. T.
VHF
VLCC
VMI
V. O. W.
VOC
VPN
VSL
Vis-à-vis
WAP
WCS
WMS
W. R.
WTO
W. W.
YAS

Section 2 Logistics Practice

Problem and Reflection

Activity One:

As a logistics English teacher, you should have the basic knowledge about the famous logistics providers in the world. Read the following information, do you know the specific domain of the following ones? (http://www. inboundlogistics. com/cms/top-100-3pls/)

Top 100 3PL Providers

The Top 100 3PL Providers chart in the July 2011 issue of *Inbound Logistics* has been completely updated, augmented and expanded to position you for 2012 and beyond.

Reflecting the diverse needs of *IL* readers, and the frenetic pace of growth of the market segment, it includes well - known companies, a smattering of 3PL niche providers, and newer companies offering specialized logistics services. They're all listed alphabetically to make it solutions-based resource, rather than to rank one provider over another. Below is the list of companies featured in the Top 100 chart.

A&R Logistics

A. N. Deringer

Access America Transport

ADS Logistic Services

AFN

Agility

Americold

APL Logistics

Aspen Logistics

Barrett Distribution Centers

BDP International

Bender Group

Big Dog Logistics

BNSF Logistics

C. H. Robinson Worldwide

Cardinal Logistics

CaseStack

Caterpillar Logistics Services

CEVA Logistics
ChemLogix
Columbian Logistics Network
Comprehensive Logistics
Corporate Traffic
Crowley Logistics
CRST Logistics
CT Logistics
CTSI-Global

Damco
Distribution Technology
DSC Logistics
Dupré Logistics

Echo Global Logistics
England Logistics
Evans Distribution Systems
Exel/DHL Supply Chain
Expeditors

FAC Logistics
FedEx SupplyChain

Genco ATC
Geodis Wilson
Greatwide Logistics Services

Hellmann Worldwide Logistics

Inmar

J. B. Hunt Transport Services
Jacobson Companies
Johanson Transportation Service

Kane Is Able
Kelron Logistics
Kenco Logistic Services
Kontane Logistics
Kuehne+Nagel

Landstar System
LeSaint Logistics
LINC Logistics Company
Logistics Management Solutions (LMS)
Lynden
LynnCo Supply Chain Solutions

Mallory Alexander
Matson Logistics
Menlo Worldwide Logistics
MIQ Logistics

New Breed Logistics
Nexus
NFI

Odyssey Logistics
OHL

Panalpina
Penske Logistics
Performance Team
Pilot Freight Services
Port Jersey Logistics

Regal Logistics
RMX Global Logistics
RR Donnelley
RSI Logistics

Ruan

Ryder Supply Chain Solutions

Saddle Creek Corporation

Schenker AG

SEKO Logistics

Serec of California

Shippers Warehouse

Strive Logistics

TMSi Logistics

TransGroup Worldwide Logistics

Transplace

Tucker Company Worldwide

UniGroup Worldwide Logistics

Union Pacific Distribution Services

Unyson Logistics

UPS

UTi Services

Vantix Logistics

Wagner Industries

Weber Logistics

Werner Enterprises/Werner Global Logistics

Wheels Clipper

WSI (Warehouse Specialists Inc.)

Yusen Logistics

Activity Two:

Efficiency is one standard for the logistics service. Read the following article about "logistics strategy" and then visited one logistics company with the question "Has the company created a logistics strategy?" (http://logistics. about. com/od/supplychainin-troduction/a/strategy. htm)

Creating a Logistics Strategy

What Is a Logistics Strategy?

When a company creates a logistics strategy it is defining the service levels at which its logistics organization is at its most cost effective. Because supply chains are constantly changing and evolving, a company may develop a number of logistics strategies for specific product lines, specific countries or specific customers.

Why Implement a Logistics Strategy?

The supply chain constantly changes and that will affect any logistics organization. To adapt to the flexibility of the supply chain, companies should develop and implement a formal logistics strategy. This will allow a company to identify the impact of imminent changes and make organizational or functional changes to ensure service levels are not reduced.

What Is Involved in Developing a Logistic Strategy?

A company can start to develop a logistics strategy by looking at four distinct levels of their logistics organization.

Strategic: By examining the company's objectives and strategic supply chain decisions, the logistics strategy should review how the logistics organization contributes to those high-level objectives.

Structural: The logistics strategy should examine the structural issues of the logistics organization, such as the optimum number of warehouses and distribution centers or what products should be produced at a specific manufacturing plant.

Functional: Any strategy should review how each separate function in the logistics organization is to achieve functional excellence.

Implementation: The key to developing a successful logistics strategy is how it is to be implemented across the organization. The plan for implementation will include development or configuration of an information system, introduction of new policies and procedures and the development of a change management plan.

Components to Examine when Developing a Logistics Strategy

When examining the four levels of logistics organization, all components of the operation should be examined to ascertain whether any potential cost benefits can be achieved. There are different component areas for each company but the list should at least include the following:

Transportation: Does the current transportation strategies help service levels?

Outsourcing: What outsourcing is used in the logistics function? Would a partnership with a third party logistics company improve service levels?

Logistics Systems: Do the current logistics systems provide the level of data that is required to successfully implement a logistics strategy or are new systems required?

Competitors: Review what the competitors offer. Can changes to the company's customer service improve service levels?

Information: Is the information that drives the logistics organization real-time and accurate? If the data is inaccurate then the decisions that are made will be in error.

Strategy Review: Are the objectives of the logistics organization in line with company objectives and strategies?

A successfully implemented logistics strategy is important for companies who are dedicated to keeping service levels at the highest levels possible despite changes that occur in the supply chain.

Activity Three:

With your training experience as a logistics English teacher, read the following article and try to draw the process chart of the logistics system.

Components of a Logistics System

A logistics system can be made up of many different functional activities, some of which are described briefly below:

1) *Customer Service* Customer service includes a wide set of activities that attempt to keep a customer satisfied with a product or service. The three primary elements of customer service include pre-transaction, transaction, and post-transaction activities.

2) *Purchasing* Most organizations include purchasing as a major supply chain activity.

Purchasing does not take a financial genius to realize the impact that suppliers can have on a firm's total cost. Furthermore, many features that make their way into final products originate with suppliers. Supplier capabilities can help differentiate a producer's final goods or service.

3) *Inbound Transportation* Larger organizations usually have a specialized traffic and transportation function to manage the physical and informational links between the supplier and the buyer. For some organizations, transportation is the single largest category of supply chain costs, especially for highly diversified organizations. While a firm may have minimal common purchase requirements between its operating units, opportunities usually exist to coordinate the purchase of transportation services.

4) *Quality Control* Quality control has taken on increased importance during the

last 15 years. Almost all organizations recognize the importance of supplier quality and the need to prevent rather than simply detect quality problems. The emphasis has shifted from detecting defects at the time of receipt or use to prevention early in the materials: sourcing process. Progressive organizations work directly with suppliers to develop proper quality control procedures and processes.

5) *Demand and Supply Planning* Demand planning identifies all the claims (or demand) on output. This includes forecasts of anticipated demand, inventory adjustments, orders taken but not filled and spare part and after-market requirements. Supply planning is the process of taking demand data and developing a supply, production, and logistics net-work capable of satisfying demand requirements.

6) *Receiving, Materials Handling, and Storage* All inbound material must be physically received as it moves from a supplier to a purchaser. In a non - JIT environment, material must also be stored or staged. Receiving, materials handling, and storage are usually part of the materials management function because of the need to control the physical processing and handling of inventory.

7) *Material or Inventory Control* The terms material control and inventory control are sometimes used interchangeably. Within some organizations, however, these terms have different meanings. The material control group is often responsible for managing material releases to suppliers. This includes generating the release, contacting a supplier directly concerning changes, and monitoring the status of inbound shipments. Material control activities are sometimes the responsibility of the purchasing department, particularly in smaller organizations. The inventory control group is often responsible for determining the inventory level of finished goods required to support customer requirements, which emphasizes the physical distribution (i. e., outbound or downstream) side of the supply chain. Integrated supply chain management requires that the material and inventory control groups coordinate their efforts to ensure a smooth and uninterrupted flow to customers.

8) *Order Processing* Order processing helps ensure that customers receive material when and where they require it. Problems with order processing have involved accepting orders before determining if adequate production capacity is available, not coordinating

order processing with order scheduling, and using internal production dates rather than the customer's preferred date to scheduling, and using internal production dates rather than the customer's preferred date to schedule the order. Order processing is an important part of supply chain management: it represents a link between the producer and the external customer.

9) *Production Planning, Scheduling, and Control* These activities involve determining a time-phased schedule of production, developing short-term production schedules, and controlling work-in-process production. The production plan often relies on forecasts from marketing to estimate the volume of materials that are required over the near term. Because operation is responsible for carrying out the production plan and meeting customer order due dates, order processing, production planning, and operations must work together closely.

10) *Warehousing/Distribution* Before a product heads to the customer, it may be stored for a period in a warehouse or distribution center. This is particularly true for companies that produce according to a forecast in anticipation of future sales. Increasingly, as companies make a product only after receiving a customer order, this part of the supply chain may become less important.

11) *Shipping* This activity involves physically getting a product ready for distribution to the customer. This requires packing to prevent damage, completing any special labeling requirements, completing the required shipping documents, or arranging transportation with an approved carrier. For obvious reasons, shipping and outbound transportation must work together closely.

12) *Outbound Transportation* Fewer organizations "own" the transportation link to their customers than was the case just a few years ago. Increasingly, full-service transportation providers are designing and managing entire distribution networks for their clients.

The process chart of the logistics system:

Answer（Activity Three：Section 1）

3PL 3rd Party Logistics 第三方物流

4PL 4th Party Logistics 第四方物流

AAR Association of American Railroads 美国铁路协会

4SC 4-High Straddle Carrier 集装箱高跨车吊具

ACI Advance Commercial Information 商业预报信息

AEO Authorized Economic Operators 授权经济运营商

AMS Automated Manifest System 海关自动舱单系统

ALC Australian Logistics Council 澳大利亚物流委员会

APEC Asia-Pacific Economic Cooperation 亚太经济合作组织

APS Automatic Planning and Scheduling 自动计划时间编制

API Application Programming Interface 程序设定界面

ARENA Asia North America Eastbound Rate Agreement 亚洲北美东向运输协会

AS/RS Automated Storage and Retrieval System 自动化存储和修复系统操作

AWB Air Waybill 空运提单

ASEAN Association of South East Asian Nations 东盟

API Application Programming Interface 程序设定界面

B2B Business to Business 企业与企业间的交易

B2C Business to Customer 企业与客户间的交易

BAF Bunker Adjustment Factor 燃油附加费

B/B Break Bulk 散件杂货

BCO Beneficial Cargo Owner 货物拥有者权益

BIFA British International Freight Association 英国国际货运协会

BIMCO The Baltic and International Maritime Council 波罗的海国际海运公会

B/L Bill of Lading 海运提单

BPM Business Process Management 商业过程管理

BPO Business Process Outsourcing 企业外判程序

CAF Currency Adjustment Factor 币值附加费

CAGR Compound Annual Growth Rate 年度联合增长率

CAP Common Agricultural Policy 欧共体共同农业政策

CBM Cubic Meter 立方米

C&F Cost and Freight 成本和运费

CC Carbon Copy 抄送

CCPIT China Council for the Promotion of International Trade
中国国际贸易促进委员会

CDC Central Distribution Center 全国配送中心

CKD Completely Knocked Down
完全拆开的,完全分解的进口整车车型的一种专有名词

CDMA Code Division Multiple Address 分发(部门)若干位址编码

CEP Courier Express Parcel 包裹寄件快递

CEPA Closer Economic Partnership Arrangement 更紧密经贸关系的安排

CFM Cubic Feet per Minute 每分钟的立方米

CFR Code of Federal Regulations 联邦规则码

COFC Container on Flatcar 集装箱集卡输送

CFS Container Freight Station 集装箱货物集散站

CGI Common Gateway Interface CGI 界面

CKD Complete Knocked Down 完全装卸

CIF Cost, Insurance and Freight 成本和运费兼付保险费

CILT The Chartered Institute of Logistics and Transport 英国特许物流运输学会

CIM The Chartered Institute of Marketing 英国特许市务学会

CIM Computer Integrated Manufacturing 计算机综合制造

CIP Carriage and Insurance Paid To 兼付指定运费及保险费

CLP Container Load Plan 集装箱装载计划表

C/O Certificate of Origin 产地来源证

C. O. C. Carrier's Own Container 船东提供集装箱

C. O. D. Cash On Delivery 交货付现

COFC Container-on-flatcar 集装箱输送

CPFR Collaborative Planning, Forecasting and Replenishment
合作计划、预测和补给

CPG Consumer Packaged Goods 生活消费品包装
CPT Carriage Paid To 兼付指定运费
CSC International Convention for Safe Container 对安全容器的国际规定
CSI Container Security Initiative 集装箱安全计划
CTN Confectioners, Tobacconists and Newsagents 糖果店、烟草店及报亭
CY Container Yard 集装箱堆场
C&F Cost and Freight 成本和运费
D/A Document Against Acceptance 承兑交单
DAF Delivery at Frontier 货交边境
DCC Dedicated Contract Carriage 专项合同运费
DDC Destination Delivery Charge 目的地提货费
DDP Delivered Duty Paid 完税后交货
DDU Delivered Duty Unpaid 未完税交货
DES Delivered Ex-Ship 货交指定港口船上
DEQ Delivered Ex-Quay 货交指定港口仓库
D. G. Dangerous Goods 危险货物
DIP Act Dip(food), a type of sauce into which food is dipped 食物被浸泡
DIY Do-It-Yourself 自己动手做
D/O Delivery Order 出货单
D/P Document Against Payment 付款交单
DPP Damage Protection Plan 集装箱损坏保险
DPWN Deutsche Post World Net 德国邮电系统网络
DRP Distribution Resources Planning 分发资源计划
D/R Dock Receipt 码头收货单
EAN European Article Number 欧洲条形码
ECR Efficient Consumer Response 有效客户响应
EDC European Distribution Center 欧洲配送中心
EDIFACT Electronic Data Interchange For Administration, Commerce and Transport 一种 EDI 标准
EBIDS E-Business Industry Development Initiatives 电子商务发展协会

EDI Electronic Data Interchange 电子资讯传递

EEC European Economic Community 欧洲经济共同体

EEZ Exclusive Economic Zone 经济特区

ELA European Logistics Association 欧洲物流协会

EMEA Europe, Middle East and Africa 欧洲、中东和非洲

EPC Electronic Product Codes 电子产品码

ERM Enterprise Resources Management 企业资源管理

ERP Enterprise Resources Planning 企业资源计划

ETD Estimated Time of Departure 预定出发时间

ETA Estimated Time of Arrival 预定到达时间

ETO Economic/Technical/Organizational 电子的,技术的,组织的

EXW Ex-Works 到户取货

FAA Federal Aviation Administration 联邦航空管理

FAF Fuel Adjustment Factor 燃料附加费

FAO Food and Agriculture Organization 联合国粮农组织

FAK Freight All Kinds 同一费率

FAS Free Alongside Ship 船边交货

FB/L FIATA Combined Transport Bill of Lading 国际运输商协会联运提单

FCL Full Container Load 整箱集装

FCR Forwarder's Cargo Receipt 货物承运人领货单

FDI Foreign Direct Investment 外国直接投资

FEFC Far East Freight Conference 远东(欧洲)运费公会

FEU Forty Feet Equivalent Unit 40 英尺标准杂装箱计算单位

FGP Factory-gate Pricing 出厂定价

F. I. Free In 船方负责装船费用

FIATA International Federation of Forwarding Agent Associations
国际货运代理协会联合会

FIFO First-in, First-out 货物先进仓和先出仓的安排

F. I. O. Free In and Out 船方不负担装卸费

FLOST Free In, Out, Stowed & Trimmed 船方不负担装船、卸船、理舱及平舱费用

FMC Federal Maritime Commission 美国联邦海事委员会

FMCG Fast-Moving Consumer Goods 快速消费品

FOB Free On Board 离岸价格

FOC Flag of Convenience 方便旗

F. O. Free Out 船方不负担卸船费用

F. O. R. Free On Rail 火车上交货

F. O. T. Free On Truck 货车上交货

F/R Flat Rack Container 平板集装箱

FRC Fuel Recovery Charge 恢复燃料费

FTAA Free Trade Area of the Americas 美洲自由贸易区

FTP File Transfer Protocol 档案传输协议

FTZ Free Trade Zones 自由贸易区

FTL Full Truck Load 整车运输

GATT General Agreement on Tariffs and Trade 关贸总协定

GDP Gross Domestic Product 国民生产总值

GRI General Rate Increasing 全部费率调高

GSA General Sales Agent 总销售代理

GSC Global Supply Chain 全球供应链

GWT Gross Weight 毛重

HAFFA Hong Kong Association of Freight Forwarding and Logistics Ltd. 香港货运物流业协会有限公司

HAWB House Air Waybill 代理行空运提单

H/H Half Height Container 半高集装箱

LASH Lighter Aboard Ship 集装箱子母船

LAN Local Area Networking 本区域网络

L/C Letter of Credit 信用证

LCL Less (than) Container Load 并箱散货

L/C Letter of Guarantee 保函

L. I. Liner Inward 入口航线

LILO Last-in, Last-out 货物后进仓和后出仓的安排

L. I. O. Liner In and Out 船方负责装卸费,但不包码头费

L. O. A. Length Overall 全长

Lo-Lo ship Lift-on Lift-off ship 吊装船

Lot-for-Lot 逐批批量法

LLP Lead Logistics Provider 精细物流提供商

LNG Liquefied Natural Gas 液化天然气

LPG Liquefied Petroleum Gas 液化石油气

LSP Logistics Service Provider 物流服务提供商

LT (Lead Time) Time between placing and receiving an order 订货到交货日期

LTL Less-Than-Truckload 散货拼车

IADA Intra Asia Discussion Agreement 亚洲集装箱运输研讨协定

I. A. Rates Independent Action Rates 独立等级价格

IATA International Air Transport Association 国际航空运输协会

IBC International Bulk Container 中型液体集装箱

ICAO International Civil Aviation Organization 国际民用航空组织

ICC International Chamber of Commerce 国际商会

ICD International Control Distribution 国际控制配送

ICP Internet Content Provider 联网内容供应商

ICT Information and Communications Technology 资讯和通信技术

ICAR Indian Council of Agricultural Research 印度农业研究委员会

IDA Infocomm Development Authority of Singapore Infocomm 新加坡发展协会

IGD Institute of Grocery Distribution 零售配送协会

IMDG International Maritime Dangerous Goods Code 国际危险商品代码

IMF International Monetary Fund 国际货币基金会

IMO International Maritime Organization 国际海事组织

Incoterm International Commercial Term 国际商务术语

IP Internet Protocol 国际网络议定书

IP Inward Processing 运进加工

IPI Interior Point Intermodal 经美国西岸入内陆运输

IPPC International Plant Protection Convention 国际植物保护协议

IRA Informal Rate Agreement 非正式运价协定

ISDN Integrated Server Digital Network 综合服务数字网络

ISO International Standard Organization 国际标准化组织

ISP Internet Service Provider 网络供应商

ISPS International Ship and Port Facility Security 国际船舶与港口保安设施规则

I. A. Rates Independent Action Rates 独立等级价格

M&A Mergers and Acquisitions 并购合同

MAI Multilateral Agreement on Investment 多边投资合约(合同)

MAWB Master Air Waybill 空运提单

MERCOSUR A Regional Trade Agreement (RTA) between Argentina, Brazil, Paraguay and Uruguay founded in 1991 by the Treaty of Asuncion.

南方共同市场

MLB Mainland Bridge 大陆桥运输模式

MLO Main Line Operators 远洋船公司

MNC Multinational Corporations 多国(跨国)公司

MOFTEC The Ministry of Foreign Trade and Cooperation 国家对外贸易合作部

MRP Material Requirements Planning 材料需要计划

MPL Marginal Product of Labor 边际劳动力产品

M/S Motor Ship 轮船

MSDS Material Safety Data Sheet 材料安全资料表

MTO Multimode Transport Operator 联运商

N/A Not Applicable/Not Available 不适用、无资料

NAFTA North American Free Trade Association 南美自由贸易协会

NAP Network Access Point 网络途径点

NFC National Freight Corporation 国营货运公司

N. O. E. Not Otherwise Enumerated 除非另有列名

N. O. S. Not Otherwise Specified 除非另有指定

NVOCC Non Vessel Operating Common Carrier 无船舶公共承运商

OCP Overland Common Point 内陆公共交货点

OECD Economic Cooperation and Development 经济合作与发展组织

OEM Original Equipment Manufacturer 原产商

O/H Over Height 超出正常高度

ORC Origin Receiving Charge 始发港附加费

O/S Open Side Container 开边集装箱

O/T Open Top Container 开顶集装箱

OTC Over the Counter 超出计数

OTIF on Time in Full 按时装载

O/W Over Width 超出正常宽度

PBOC The People's Bank of China 中国银行

PCC Processing under Customs Control 海关过程控制

PCS Port Congestion Surcharge 港口挤塞附加费

PEQ Post Entry Quarantine 后补进口检疫

P&I Club Protection and Indemnity Club 英国标准保赔会

PQ Order Positive Quality 优良品质订单

POD Port of Discharge 卸货港

POL Port of Loading 装货港

POP Point of Presence 存在的点

PPP Point-to-Point Protocol 点对点的草案

PRD Pearl River Deta 珠江三角洲

PSS Peak Season Surcharge 季节附加费

RCH Railway Clearing House 铁路清算所

RF Reefer Container 冷藏集装箱

RFI Request for Information 书面信息要求

RFP Request for Proposal 书面建议要求

RFQ Request for Quotation 书面报价要求

RFRC Rail Fuel Recovery Charge 轨道燃料恢复费用

Ro-Ro ship Roll-on Roll-off ship 滚装船

ROCE Return on Capital Employment 投资回报

ROI Return on Investment 投资回报

RRS Rate Restoration Surcharge 比率修复附加费

R/T Revenue Tons 计费吨

SAD Single Administrative Document 单独管理文档

SAN Storage Area Network 网络存储

S/C Sales Contract 销售合同

SCOR Supply-chain Operations Reference 供应链运作参考

SDR Special Drawing Right 专属权

SET Secure Electronic Transaction 安全电子交易

SKU Stock Keeping Unit 储备保持的单位

SLA Service-level Agreement 服务协议

SME Small and Medium-size Enterprises 中小型企业

S/O Shipping Order 付货通知单

S. O. C. Shipper's Own Container 付货人所属集装箱

SQL Structure Query Language 架构疑问语

S/S Steamship 汽轮船

SSL Secure Socket Layer 付款加密法

S. T. C. Said To Contain 据报内装

S/O S/I Shipping Order/Shipping Instruction 付运通知书/落货纸

TACA Transatlantic Conference Agreement 跨大西洋公会协定

TCP Transmission Control Protocol 传输控制草案

TEU Twenty-foot Equivalent Unit 20 英尺标准集装箱计算单位

T. H. C. Terminal Handling Charge 码头操作费

TMS Transportation Management System 运输管理系统

TOFC Trailer-on-Flatcar 集装箱车架输送

TQC Total Quality Control 全面品质控制

TQM Total Quality Management 全面品质管理

T. R. S. Terminal Receiving Station 码头收货站

TSA Transpacific Stabilization Agreement 跨太平洋稳定协议

T/S Transshipment Port 转口港

TSR Trans Siberian Railway 西伯利亚大铁路

TT Telegraphic Transfer 电汇

T/T Transit Time　航程

TUPE Transfer of Undertaking (Protection of Employment)　转让担保(保护使用)

TVC Time Volume Contract　时间货量合同

TWRA Transpacific Westbound Rate Agreement　泛太平洋西运费协会

UCP500 Uniform Customs and practice for Documentary Credits
跟单信用证统一惯例和实务

USDA U. S. Department of Agriculture Animal and Plant Inspection Service
美国动植物检疫局

ULCC Ultra Large Crude Carrier　50 万吨油输

UNCTAD United Nations Conference of Trade and Development　联合国贸发会议

V. A. T. Value Added Tax　增值税

VHF Very High Frequency　甚高额

VLCC Very Large Crude Carrier　20 万吨油轮

VMI Vendor Managed Inventory　供应商的存货管理系统

V. O. W. Vehicle On Wheel　可驾驶的车辆

VOC Vessel Operating Carrier　船舶承运商

VPN Virtual Private Network　虚拟网络

VSL Vessel　轮船

Vis-ὰ-vis with regard to　关于,对于

WAP Wireless Appreciation Protocol　无线应(运)用草案

WCS Wireless Communications Service　无线通信服务

WMS Warehouse Management System　仓库管理系统

W. R. ar Risks　战争险

WTO World Trade Organization　世界贸易组织

W. W. arehouse Warrant　仓单

YAS Yen Appreciate Surcharg　日元调整费

Module Four

Action Research Competence of Logistics English Teachers

Discussion:

◇ What is action research?

◇ Why do logistics English teachers do action research?

◇ How to do action research in the field of logistics English teaching?

Section 1 Understanding Action research

Problem and Reflection

Activity One: Discuss the following questions in small groups

1. What is your understanding of research?
2. According to your understanding, have you ever done any research? What is the result?

Activity Two: Reading

1. Pre-reading question:

You are going to read a text about research. Before reading it, combined with your above answers in activity one, discuss with your peers the process of research.

The process of research:

Now read the text, checking to see if your process is the same with the heroine in this text:

Ms. Jiang has just bought a new handbag. It is so cute that she loves it so much. However, on the first day of her taking it to her company, a small problem worried her. "Is it made of real leather?", "Is it made of leather?" Whenever she went, she met with this question from the curious colleague. This question also arouses her own curiosity.

With this question, she began to find the solutions. Firstly, she telephoned the handbag shop for their proof. Secondly, she recalled that she knew a leather expert and then she went to get his examination. Besides, she thought of the most uncultured yet practical way to test it. She tore one tiny string from the hidden place and fired it. From the smell of the flame, she got a conclusion. Combined with the answer she got from the above-mentioned sources, she was pleased. The cute handbag deserves the penny.

Post-reading task:

After reading the text, rearrange the following words for the process of research. (The answer is hidden somewhere in this module)

collect data ; question; assumption; test assumption; analyze

2. Read the following text written by an action researcher. (Ferrance, 2000: 22).

When I sat down to write about my experience with action research, I began by looking over my team's final report, my meeting notes, and my e-mails to our consultant from the LAB at Brown. I am glad I did. Doing action research can be a little like labor. You forget what it was really like. The notes and e-mails reminded me of the messiness of our meetings and our struggle to pare down the project into something manageable.

I am the Title I Resource Teacher for the Charlotte M. Murkland School in Lowell, Massachusetts. Our school is in the inner city and has about 530 students in pre-school to fourth grade. The Murkland has a Khmer bilingual strand and over 60% of our students are from homes in which English is not spoken. Our poverty rate is one of the highest in the city, at about 89%-92%, depending on the month. The Murkland is a new building with an experienced, stable staff that formed when the school was built six years ago. Although our school offers us many challenges, on most days, most of us are glad to be at the Murkland.

"Do you like research?" asked my Title I facilitator, Eileen Skovholt. "Yes," I said, "I loved research in college." With those words I was on my way to becoming a teacher-researcher. That conversation led to a multidisciplinary team, made up of our vice principal, the city-wide Title I facilitator, an ESL teacher, a bilingual teacher, a special education teacher, and myself, being asked to attend the LAB Institute on Cultural and Linguistic Diversity: Problem Solving through Action Research, held at Brown University.

At the conference, our group was taken with the idea that we could actually begin to conduct inquiries into our own teaching. We have so often felt pulled in one direction or another by the swing of the educational pendulum. By doing our own action research we could gain a better perspective into our own teaching and the students' learning. The changes that we would make in our teaching would come out of our own work. Perhaps most importantly, we would be working as a community of learners. During the conference, we began to talk about a group of bilingual Cambodian students in our third and fourth grades who were non-readers. Most of them were new to our school. They would, of course, be referred to special education for testing. The truth is, we see students such as these just about every year. At this age, time is short and the testing process is time-consuming. Even when the testing is completed, we still need to develop a program for them. Action research would provide us the opportunity to try different strategies and see which ones actually brought about significant change for our students. After visiting Brown, we were invited to write the grant that led to this project. Several of us had never worked together before. The discussion that occurred as we were writing the grant generated many ideas. As we wrote the grant, there was a sense of common goals and a feeling that what we were about to do was important to our school and to our own personal growth.

Our Approach

Our research question became, "What can we provide for effective reading instruction for third- and fourth-grade English language learners who are limited readers or nonreaders?" We began the literature research project by gathering articles that we felt would be of interest. We each read the articles and set aside a day to report our findings back to the group.

We also collected as much information as possible on our target students. We looked at their past records and at their current programs.

Then we had to determine where we would go from here. This was the most difficult time for our team. Up to this point we seemed to have moved along with only a few problems. Now, our meetings seemed to go in circles. We became very frustrated with our lack of progress. Our impatience caused discord among the members of the team. We were able to move past this point by allowing each member to choose a different strategy to research. We chose among strategies that we had either discussed or read about, and then worked with a targeted group of students. Each teacher collected data and then looked to see how her own practice might be improved. In retrospect, this was a good decision. Looking at your own teaching is real professional development.

Working with the Students

My part in the project was to work each morning with two of our target fourth-grade students. They would sit with me at the computer and we would write a few sentences about what they were doing in school. This became a newspaper that was sent home to parents. Students had to read what they wrote to their parents and the parents had to sign the newspaper and return it to school. In later editions, we began to have students ask the parents for feedback.

As students sat with me and we talked, I was able to help them build and write sentences in English. The process was easy and non-threatening. We also talked about vocabulary and what concepts they were learning in their other content areas. We wrote articles to inform their parents about this. The concept of how to use a pulley is the same in any language.

Findings

What makes action research so powerful? As a team, we interviewed our students and asked for their views on which of our strategies helped them to become stronger readers. It is powerful to listen to students. Even as seasoned teachers, we can make wrong assumptions about how a child is learning. A staff member from the LAB at Brown helped us to do a linguistic analysis of the students' comments. For me, this was the most interesting piece. We looked at all the student comments and then charted their responses. For example, we counted how many times they talked about needing to obtain support from a Khmer speaking teacher. What they said made perfect sense. They needed the most support when their English skills were less developed. This need lessened as they became better English speakers. For us, this supported our own feelings that a few words in Khmer at the right time can make a big difference in their learning. For my own research piece, it was good to learn that most of the parents liked and enjoyed reading the newspaper. By the end of the project, parents began to request articles.

Helping Parents to be Involved with Their Child's Learning

The newspaper was a wonderful way to communicate with our parents about what their children were learning. By having the students write the articles, they were reinforcing their own learning and they were practicing English. Therefore, the student newspaper was a viable idea to teach English sentence structure, reinforce vocabulary, reinforce content skills and information, and communicate with parents.

The one common finding from everyone's research was that students needed to have their lessons supported in Khmer. As they are learning English, they need to be able to go back to their first language to have their learning verified.

Action research allows us the opportunity to shape and refine our own teaching and to build on our own successes.

In a climate that is at best stressful, action research allows a teacher to focus her energy in a positive way. So many of the issues in education today are out of our hands. As education continues through the reform process, teachers must have a say in how they change their own practices. I found that action research was a process that helped me to put some of my assumptions to the test. I made unexpected discoveries about my own teaching by listening carefully to students. Action research changes the conversations that take place in a school. This has an incredible effect on the school climate for staff and children.

Need for Professional Educational Researchers

When doing action research it is vital to have the input of professional researchers. They can bring a perspective and experience to the work that is invaluable. Their presence in the project helps to legitimize that work. With their involvement there is an increased chance that the work will play a role in school or district priorities. Our consultants aided us by helping us to refine our question, establish an action plan and timetable, and reflect on our data to find trends or patterns. Our consultants were able to give us that third-party perspective and reassure us that our work and pace were on target.

Post-reading task:

a) Choose from the following list the characteristics of action research. (The answer is hidden somewhere in this module)

critical self-reflection; small scale; about learning why we do certain things; collaboration; a library project where we learn more about a topic that interests us; funds by the government; practical concern; bring about a change;

b) The process of doing action research is similar with that of doing research. Can you find the slight difference? Read the following figure and discuss with your peers to explain the process of doing action research.

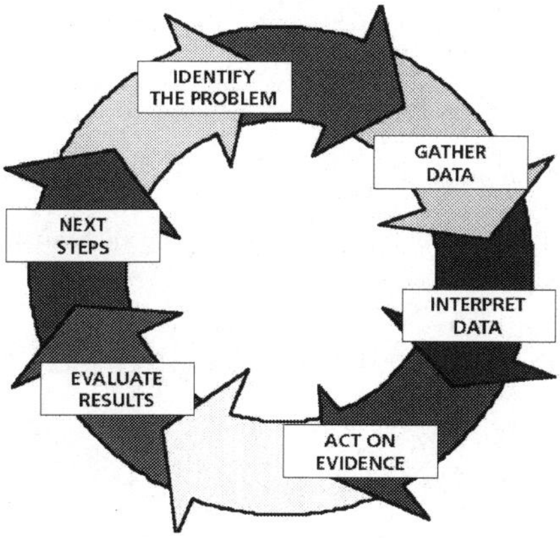

(**Cited from Ferrance, 2000: 15**)

Activity Three: Discussion for the reasons of doing action research

Make a list of your reasons for doing action research. The benefits may for the English teachers and for the students. The reasons you mention could be professional development for the teachers and interest for the students, etc.

1. What are the reasons for doing action research?

For the students	For English teachers

2. After you finish this list, discuss your ideas in small groups of three or four. As a group decide what the three most popular reasons are, both for the English teachers and the students.

Voice from the Theory

DEFINITION:

Typically, action research is undertaken in a school setting. It is a reflective process that allows for inquiry and discussion as components of the "research." Often, action research is a collaborative activity among colleagues searching for solutions to everyday, real problems experienced in schools, or looking for ways to improve instruction and increase student achievement. Rather than dealing with the theoretical, action research allows practitioners to address those concerns that are closest to them, ones over which they can exhibit some influence and make change. (Peter et al., 1994)

Section 2 Doing Action Research

Problem and Reflection

Activity One: Lead-in knowledge

1. Now you are going to do an action research, how do you select the topic? (List the possible ways of selecting topics, the first two choices have been given.)

How to select a topic:
— Choose a topic by general reading
— Choose a topic by observing & critical thinking of the teaching behavior
—
—
—
—

2. The process of selecting and developing a topic is done by asking some questions. Match the questions on the left side with the procedure on the right side (the answer is hidden somewhere in this module).

a. How long have you got to do the research? Is there a deadline for its completion?	A. Purpose
b. What is the likely outcome of the research, as you intend it?	B. Topic
c. Why are you engaging in this action research?	C. Focus
d. What area are you going to investigate?	D. Product
e. How are you going to conduct the research?	E. Mode
f. As you proceed with your research, do you suppose you will have to rethink your original question?	F. Timing
g. What is the precise question you are going to ask yourself within that area?	G. Resources
h. What are the resources, both human and material, that you can call upon to help you complete the research?	H. Refocusing/fine-tuning

3. The following are some possible ways in collecting the data when doing action research. Read and decide which is familiar and which is rather new to you and your peers. Select the two regularly used methods in your action research.

interview; questionnaire; verbal reports; observation; case studies; evaluation

Activity Two: Reading

Read the following description about questionnaire and interview (Wallace, 1998). Think about the pros and cons of both.

We use questionnaires and interviews when we want to tap into the knowledge, opinions, ideas and experiences of our learners, fellow teachers, parents or whatever. We do this by asking questions. The answers are usually recorded in some way so that they become available for subsequent reflection and analysis. In questionnaires, the questions are usually set out in a very systematic way, and very often the questionnaire is answered by reading the questions, and then ticking responses, or writing in short answers. Interviews are by definition oral, more like conversations. Very often, though, in surveys (especially large-scale surveys) the questions asked orally are read aloud by the interviewer from a questionnaire. Interviews that are not of the survey type, on the other hand, can be quite free-wheeling and open-ended so the term 'interview' can cover quite a wide range of interaction from something like a spoken questionnaire at one end of the scale to something very like a conversation between professionals at the other.

Post-reading task: Discussion.

Discuss the differences between the questionnaire and interview. Fill in the blanks for the differences. (The first has been given)

Questionnaire	*Interview*
No emotion	*Have tone/feeling/emotion*

Activity Three: Discussion of observation techniques

Classroom observation is also much used in doing action research. With the clear focused objectives to the observation (ourselves as teachers; our students; the context), some possible methods are used in recording. Read the following descriptions of the methods and in a group guess the terms used. The answer is hidden somewhere in this module)

a) This means that the observation is observed and analyzed as the teaching/learning actually happens without using any electronic means of recalling the data. This can be done by marking checklists or simply taking notes. __________

b) It is worth remembering that much interaction can be recorded using a small portable cassette recorder. Sometimes cheap recording machines are more appropriate than more sensitive advanced machines, as several can be used at a time, and also more sophisticated machines are sometimes more difficult to operate. Using a small cassette recorder is, of course, most effective in one-to-one teaching situations, or with small group work. ____________

c) This is the most intrusive technique, but with the development of 'palmcorders' and similar hand-held video recorders, it has become much less so. The justification of the extra expense and inconvenience of this method is that it can make a permanent record of contextual and paralinguistic data, such as chalkboard work, the layout of the classroom, movement, gestures, facial expressions, and so on. Remember, also, that this method is selective: you can't capture everything. ____________

d) The problem with both the method b) and c) described is that, although they provide rich data on a permanent-recall basis, specific items of data may not be very accessible. Also data only on tape are not amenable to certain kinds of analysis (e. g. detailed discourse analysis). It is very often the case, therefore, that material which has been recorded then has to be written down according to the recording. This is a very time-consuming business. ____________

Voice from the Theory

■ The idea of using research in a "natural" setting to change the way that the researcher interacts with that setting can be traced back to Kurt Lewin, a social psychologist and educator whose work on action research was developed throughout the 1940s in the United States. "Lewin is credited with coining the term 'action research' to describe work that did not separate the investigation from the action needed to solve the problem" (McFarland & Stansell, 1993: 14).

(Answer:

The process of research: question ⟶ assumption ⟶ collect data ⟶ analyze

⟶test assumption)

(Answer:

The characteristics of action research: critical self – reflection; small scale; collaboration; practical concern; bring about a change)

(Answer:

The process of selecting and developing a topic: A–c; B–d;

(Answer:

Observation techniques: a): real time observation b): audio taping c): video taping d): transcription)

Section 3 Questionnaires

Problem and Reflection

Activity One: Knowledge of questionnaire

1. Make a list of questionnaires being used as a method in collecting data. The utilized questionnaires may either in your daily life or in the research work.

Questionnaires used in your daily life	Questionnaires used by the researchers
e. g.	e. g.

2. After you finish this list, discuss your ideas in small groups of three or four. As a group decide which is most difficult in the procedures of using questionnaires in research. Mark the one (√) you agreed to be most difficult.

Designing questionnaires	
Using questionnaires	
Analyzing questionnaires	

Activity Two: Reading

Pre-reading task:

While using questionnaires in doing research, what sorts of problems have you met? How do you solve them? Now read a dialogue took place between two English teachers in China talking about questionnaires.

Arne: Hi, Edie. Long time no see! I heard that you have been doing action research for the past few months. How's everything going?

Edie: The action research was not so successful as I had thought before the research was done. I met a lot of difficulties in collecting data.

Arne: What instruments did you use in collecting data?

Edie: Questionnaires.

Arne: That was a very practical method in collecting data. It is economical because many testees can answer the questionnaires at the same time. Besides, analyzing the data gathered in this way is simple and easy to operate.

Edie: I think so. That's also the reason why I chose questionnaires in collecting data. However, I still got some problems.

Arne: What are the problems?

Edie: I delivered the questionnaires to some of my previous students and some of my colleagues. I thought these people might be helpful. Whereas, the students who sent back the questionnaires were only 20% of the whole I posted to. My colleagues were always too busy to give me feedback. Their smiling attitudes gave me no help at all. I waited for almost two months in collecting the questionnaires. Among them, one fifth was not useful in analyzing data. The low rate of feedback made me fail this procedure of the research. I tried to remedy it by adding some interviews to the testees. It wasted me a lot of time in collecting data. The analyzing statistics was not so reliable.

Arne: Yeah. That was just the cons of using questionnaires. The feedback rate is often low. You need to think of ways in overcoming it. Only when you have utilized an effective instrument, your research might be successful.

Edie: Thank you a lot for hearing my difficulties and giving me the suggested opinions. After meeting some frustration, I think I will know how to do next time.

Post-reading task:

Read the following statements. Decide which should be done (mark "√") and which should be avoided wherever possible (mark "×") in designing a questionnaire. (The answer is hidden somewhere in this module.)

- Asking questions which involve the respondent in a lot of effort (e.g. seeking out information not readily available) ( )
- Keep each question short, simple unambiguous and pertinent to its respondent. ( )
- Phrase each question as precisely as possible. ( )
- Using unfamiliar, difficult and too many words ( )
- Using double-barreled questions (two questions in one) ( )
- Asking questions which use the terms 'regularly' 'occasionally' 'usually' and 'normally' ( )
- Asking unnecessary personal questions ( )

Activity Three: Discussion

1. Examine the following two examples of questionnaires. Decide which is closed and which is open question. Find the differences and the situation they individually suit. (Wallace: 135)

Example 1 (Please tick (√) the appropriate box.) How many years have you been studying English? 0-3 □   4-6 □   7-10 □   more than 10 □

Example 2 Why did you decide to learn English rather than some other foreign language? (If you have several reasons, pick the most important.)

2. In a group of three or four, design one questionnaire with the aim "to investigate......", using either closed questions or open questions. Change the designed questionnaire with another group. Find the inaccuracy and correct it.

Tips:

Designed questionnaires must be piloted before being used in large scale.

Voice from the Theory

DEFINITION:

What is a questionnaire? According to Richards et al. (1998: 380), a questionnaire is a set of questions on a topic or group of topics designed to be answered by a respondent. Other formats for questionnaires include check lists and rating scales. Designing questionnaires which are valid, reliable and unambiguous is a very important issue. Questionnaires are used in many branches of applied linguistics, such as in language surveys, the study of attitudes and motivation, and in needs analysis.

DESIGNING QUESTIONNAIRES

The following examples offer some forms of designing questionnaires:

1. Likert Scale: To show attitude towards one statement:

   e. g. strongly disagree   disagree   unknown   agree   strongly agree

2. Semantic differential: Two antonyms are put in distance by 5 markers. The respondent needs to choose one marker to show the attitude towards something.

   e. g. Learning English language:

   useful /______/______/______/______/______/useless

3. Background investigation: This information is very useful in analyzing questionnaire.

   e. g. 1. You were born in ____________________.

Section 4 Interviews

Problem and Reflection

Activity One: Lead-in knowledge

Like questionnaires, interviews come in many different forms, but it is most helpful to think of interviews as falling into three broad categories, namely *structured*, *unstructured* and *semi-structured*. Read the following descriptions. Write down the corresponding terms in brackets.

1. Not entirely free talk—have a research purpose in mind when initiating the interview; the interviewer must know that he or she is taking part in an interview, and should preferably also know what the purpose of the interview is. ( )
2. (Least useful) With interview questions, questionnaire is very rigid. You are running after the agenda, limiting. ( )
3. You have a list of questions about general areas, you let the interview cover you agenda. As group, pairs, or individual. People can be interviewed by 'insider' and or 'outsider'. It can be used by video, tape cassettes or notes taking. ( )

Activity Two: Reading (Wallace, 1998:153)

This article describes two interviews between the author and Japanese speakers of English as a second language. The interviewees were men on long-term job assignment in South East Asia. The initial aims of the interviews were to determine the uses to which the interviewees put English; to identify the conditions under which they used English; and to characterize in general terms their life styles while living and working outside Japan. However, the results were also found to be interesting in relation to the interviewees' second-language learning strategies in general, and in relation to certain implications of those strategies for classroom content and methodology.

The two interviews were with Mr. J. and Mr. S. , two businessmen in different offices in Singapore who had both lived and worked in Singapore for three years...

Interview one

Mr. J. never used English in his office, as all his associates were Japanese or Japanese speakers. In his free time, he usually associated with them or other members of the Japanese-speaking community. He spoke Japanese at home with his family. His uses of English were limited to business conversations with local clients and to very rare golf games with them. His other uses of English were restricted to conversations with restaurant employees, parking attendants, ticket clerks, and so on. All his information about business and current affairs was obtained through Japanese. He did not have local friends, nor did he associate with the local people or culture. He had not studied English since university. Nevertheless he claimed that, to his surprise, his level of English had not improved in the three years he had been in Singapore. He mentioned that his job was stressful due to his lack of English, and he was looking forward to returning to Japan.

Interview two

By contrast, the second businessman, Mr. S. , worked in an office with all Singaporeans. He spoke only English in all his working contacts. Both he and his Japanese wife had Singaporean friends and associated mostly with them, speaking English with them. Mr. And Mrs. S. both made exclusive use of English-language sources of information and entertainment and were trying to learn and improve their English through their own efforts. Mr. S. reported that his English had improved 'somewhat' in his three years. He enjoyed living and working abroad, and said he had no language-related problems with his work.

...

Activity Three: Discussion

While reading articles about interview, we find that some are very successful with a lot of information, whereas some are very dull. Have you ever thought of the effective strategies in using interviews? Discuss with your peers to find as many answers as possible.

Effective strategies in using interviews：
– *Don't talk/tell your own opinions. Try not to be communicative.*
– *Try to make them comfortable and relaxed, by starting the general chat.*
–
–
–
–

Voice from the Theory

■ DEFINITION：

What is an interview? According to Richards et al. (1998:236), an interview is a directed conversation between an investigator and an individual or group of individuals in order to gather information. Interviews are used to gather data for linguistic analysis and may be used in needs analysis.

Section 5 Action Research of Logistics English Teaching

Problem and Reflection

Activity One：Lead-in knowledge

The common problems of logistics English teaching will be brainstormed by your discussion. Write down your answers briefly and pick out the urgent one for you.

Problems in logistics English teaching：
—
—
—
—
—
—
The urgent problem for my logistics English teaching：

Activity Two:

Design your own action research to solve your own problem in teaching.

Activity Three:

Discuss with other logistics English teachers about the process and procedures of your action research to get peer support and suggestions.

Bibliography

Johnson, K. , Johnson, H. 1999. *Encyclopedic Dictionary of Applied Linguistics: A Handbook for Language Teaching* [M]. Blackwell Publishers Ltd.

McFarland, K. P. , & Stansell, J. C. 1993. Historical perspectives. In L. Patterson, C. M. Santa, C. G. Short, & K. Smith (Eds.) [A]. *Teachers are researchers: Reflection and action* [C]. Newark, DE: International Reading Association.

Peter, B. , Erica, B. , Ian, p. , Maye, T. , & Carol, T. 1994. Action research[J]. *Qualitative Methods in Psychology: A research guide.* Buckingham, Open University Press.

Richards, J. C. , Platt, J. , Platt, H. (Ed.). 1998. *Longman Dictionary of Language Teaching & Applied Linguistics* [M]. Beijing: Addison Longman China Limited.

Wallace, M. J. 1998. *Action research for Language Teachers* [M]. Cambridge University Press.

Module Five

Assessment and Evaluation Competence of Logistics English Teachers

Discussion:

◇ Why should the logistics English teachers carry out evaluation?

◇ What should be evaluated?

◇ How to do evaluation for the logistics English teachers?

Section 1 Understanding Evaluation Competence

Problem and Reflection

Activity One: Discuss and fill in the activity card

The evaluation competency enables the English language teachers to:
● Analyze a situation for improvement.
● Develop an attitude of constant (informal and formal) evaluation.
● Use a variety of strategies for evaluation purposes.
●
●
●
●
●

Activity Two: Reading

Pre-reading question: The following is a list of things that should be evaluated by an English language teacher. Choose the one you think most difficult and explain the reason.

√ *Evaluation of curricula*

√ *Evaluation of course books or materials evaluation*

√ *Evaluation to the students*

√ *Self-evaluation as English language teachers*

Read the following article "About Evaluation" (http://www.whitestag.org/resources). Ready to answer the questions: Why is evaluation important? How to develop an evaluation attitude? When do we evaluate? Who ought to evaluate?

Ask a Patrol Member Development candidate at the end of the summer camp, "When do you evaluate?" and he'll tell you, "Always."

Ask another candidate from Patrol Leader Development "what do you look for when you evaluate?" and he'll say, "The strong and the weak points, possible improvements, and things to keep."

Ask a third candidate, a young woman from Troop Leader Development, bowed under a large pack, "What is evaluation?" and she'll tell you everything the others have said and add, "We evaluate how well the group is keeping itself together and how well we're getting the job done."

Evaluation is a continual process, either informal or formal, of judging a situation against a standard.

Evaluation is, in essence, two things:

An attitude of continuous striving for higher goals.

A process for judging an individual's or group's completion of a task against previously identified standards.

Our desire is to improve our evaluation skills so that we evaluate in the same manner an eagle soars on the winds: constantly testing, consciously and unconsciously, wind current, flow, our altitude, strength, time, direction, position relative to our target, etc., all the elements that affect our reaching and surpassing the next mountain peak.

Why is evaluation important? Because we want to know whether we are achieving our goals. So why are goals important?

Better to ask, "What would ever be accomplished if no one ever had a goal?" What if Henry Ford had not set a goal to mass produce a car? Surely, you say, someone else would have. But only if they too had a goal.

Knowing Our Motives and Our Motivations

To achieve a goal you need a motive.

A motive is an internal force, what drives us forward, an intrinsic force within us that makes us get up earlier and go to bed later because we want to make something happen.

A motivation is an external, extrinsic reward for achieving our goals.

The thing you want to accomplish—your dream or vision—is what binds your motive and motivation together.

Something bigger than the individual is required to drive us unrelentingly towards the perceived end. Motives may be externally or internally derived. Some people are motivated by the idea of financial independence and work many years to achieve it. Others may be spurred on by the desire to be of service, to give back that which was previously rendered to them by others.

The power of a person with a goal who is convinced of the righteousness of the idea should not be underestimated. Mountains can be moved when a person's heart and mind is fully engaged in pursuit of a worthy goal.

Helping Build Self-esteem

We strive to not only provide the learner with a tool box of leadership skills but with a chest of self-esteem, to not only help the user improve his hand and head skills, but his heart as well. Thus a key part of our challenge is to tap into individual and group motives, to help them develop worthy goals.

So we set ourselves to the task of writing goals and objectives that are explicit and comprehensive, including not only the hand and head skills, but the heart skills as well. We strive to develop objectives that quantify the spirit of the White Stag Youth Leadership Development Program.

This chapter describes how to write goals and objectives that include hand, head, and heart behaviors, and how to conceive, construct, implement, and evaluate the learners' success in achieving them.

The evaluation attitude is a "predisposition to continually examine and analyze our efforts." Evaluation is a critical component of the cyclical learning process. It does not just occur formally at the conclusion of activities, but informally as well, by all involved, throughout the project or task. The evaluation attitude is one of the principals that form the basis of the White Stag Leadership Development Program.

"One who applies this attitude or technique will be continually aware of the objectives of his learnings and will attempt to measure his growth toward them."

Growth in and improvement of leadership performance are dependent upon the leader's willingness to change, his ability to define the kind of change he needs, and the experience he has in changing himself.

The leader's ability to define the kind of change he needs is based on his competency to evaluate. Changes or learning in the desired direction can be brought about only by continuous self-analysis by evaluating goals and achievements. Learning to analyze, evaluate, and plan improvement becomes, then, an objective of great significance.

Continually Applying Evaluation

Techniques and methods of evaluation are being used intensively at virtually every step of the White Stag program. Evaluation becomes second nature to the leader-in-training and it is applied as an attitude and as a learned technique to each individual's on-the-job performance.

The development of an evaluation attitude, therefore, is another key criterion in the White Stag method. Throughout the entire program numerous devices should be used to evaluate oneself, your group, or the program in its entirety. Self, peer and group rating forms, performance ratings, observation and program analysis reports and trainee and trainer evaluation scales are used frequently, both by the leaders-in-training and staff members. This technique is valuable in sharpening the candidate's awareness of what constitutes critical behavior as well as supplying motivation and guidance for further growth.

Why do we evaluate?

In a nutshell, to better ourselves and a situation.

When do we evaluate?

Informally, all the time. Formally, preferably in writing, immediately after we finish major tasks.

Who ought to evaluate?

Everyone. The leader will make it a point to informally evaluate at all times. All members will contribute to the formal (group) evaluation as a task concludes.

Voice from the Theory

DEFINITION:

Assessment (Richards, 1998:28) —— The measurement of the ability of a person or the quality or success of a teaching course, etc. Assessment may be by test, interview, questionnaire, observation, etc.

Evaluation (Richards, 1998: 163) —— In general, the systematic gathering of information for purposes of decision making. Evaluation uses both quantitative methods, gualitative methods and value judgments. In language planning, evaluation frequently involves gathering information on patterns of language use, language ability, and attitudes towards language. In language teaching programmes, evaluation is related to decisions to be made about the quality of the programme itself, and decisions about individuals in the programmes. The evaluation of programmes may involve the study of curriculum, objectives, materials, and tests or grading systems. The evaluation of individuals involves decisions about entrance to programmes, placement, progress, and achievement. In evaluating both programmes and individuals, tests and other measures are frequently used.

Section 2 From Testing to Assessment and Evaluation

Problem and Reflection

Activity One:

Read the following descriptions about authentic assessment. (Hart 1994: 9; O'Malley and Pierce 1996: 6.) Then decide, "What is your understanding of authentic assessment?"

- Authentic assessment refers to the procedures for evaluating learner progress using activities and tasks that integrate classroom goals, curricula and instruction and real-life performance.
- Authentic assessment emphasizes the communicative meaningfulness of evaluation and the commitment to measure that which we value in education.
- Authentic assessment uses the diverse forms of assessment that reflect student learning, achievement, motivation and attitudes on instructionally-relevant classroom activities.
- Authentic assessment corresponds to and mirrors good classroom practices.

- Authentic assessment's results can be used to improve instruction, based on the knowledge of learner progress.
- Authentic assessment also emphasizes the importance of the teacher's professional judgment and commitment to enhancing student learning.
- The use of self-assessment promotes the learner's direct involvement in learning and the integration of cognitive abilities with affective learning.
- My understanding: Authentic assessment is ____
____
____.

Activity Two: Reading

Read the following article about "school-based assessment" adapted from Wood (1993:71). Do you agree with the strengths and deficiencies the article stated?

School-based assessment is to test 'aspects of attainment which may not easily or adequately be tested by (final) papers' (Secondary Examinations Council, SEC 1985: 2). In affirming that school-based examining can do what one-off external examining report (McGaw et al. 1984) saw the strengths of school-based assessments to be that they:

can be used on a substantial sample of student performance, over time and over the full range of the syllabus requirements;

can assess aspects of a course not accessible to external examination.

The report went on:

We recognize, however, that school assessments can have serious deficiencies too.

We see these to be that the assessments:

can be biased for or against a student by the relationship between teacher and student;

can, in some cases, take undue account of early performance in a course and, relatively, too little of the level a student finally reaches;

can change the relationship between teacher and student by casting the teacher in the role of judge instead of that of supporter in the preparation for external assessment;

Can be undertaken with variable criteria from school to school.

Activity Three: Discussion

The development in evaluation can be highlighted by comparing authentic assessment with traditional standard testing. Standardized tests are usually based on multiple choice items, fill-in items and short, restricted-response tasks. They are administered to large numbers of testees with consistent scoring results and thus a high degree of reliability. The need to go beyond the standardized tests has recently given prominence to the concept of "alternative" assessment.

Read the following figure, comparing with the standardized testing, discuss in a group to find the corresponding items in authentic assessment. (The answer is hidden somewhere in this module)

Standardized testing	Authentic assessment
1. Testing and instruction are regarded as separate activities	1.
2. Students are treated in a uniform way	2.
3. Decisions are based on single sets of data (test scores)	3.
4. Emphasis on weakness / failures: what students cannot do	4.
5. One-shot exams	5.
6. Cultural/social-economic status bias	6.
7. Focus on one 'right answer'	7.
8. Judgment without suggestions for improvement	8.
9. Pressures teachers to narrow teaching to what is tested	9.
10. Focus on lower-order knowledge and skills	10.
11. Forbids students to interact; promotes comparisons between students (norm-referencing)	11.
12. Extrinsic learning for a grade	12.

Section 3 Evaluation to the Logistics Majors

Problem and Reflection

Activity One:

Authentic assessment includes communicative performance assessment, language portfolios and various forms of self-assessment by learners. The following summary provides a list of the basic types of authentic assessment in language learning (O'Malley and Piece 1996:12). Read and decide which type you have ever used in evaluating your students' logistics English learning. What advantages and disadvantages did you find in using it?

— oral interviews(of learners by the teacher)
— story or text retelling(with listening or reading inputs)
— writing samples(with a variety of topics and registers)
— projects and exhibitions(presentation of a collaborative effort)
— experiments and demonstrations(with oral or written reports)
— constructed-response items(to open-ended questions)
— teacher observation(of learners' work in class, making notes)
— portfolios(focused collection of learner's work to show progress)

The type I have ever used:
Advantages:
Disadvantages:

Activity Two: Reading(Arnold, 1999:286)

"Pochlio", a word originally was from Italian vocabulary— "portafoglio", is considered to be an effective method to be used by some successful teachers.

A portfolio is defined as a purposeful, selective collection of learner work and reflective self-assessment that is used to document progress and achievement over time with regard to specific criteria. In the course of the learning process the portfolio becomes a kind of autobiography of the learner.

The language portfolio combines the twin goals of the learner-centered curriculum by facilitating language learners to develop:

1. the necessary language skills and attitudes, and
2. a critical self-consciousness of their own role as active agents within the learning process, with an ability to assess their own progress and the learning arrangements.

The language portfolio serves two main functions in the total

Learning process:

— pedagogic function: a tool for self-organised language learning. Learners learn to collect authentic data of their own work, record it in suitable ways and reflect on their language learning biography.

— reporting function: a tool for reporting language learning outcomes to teachers, institutions and other relevant stakeholders (parents, administrators, other educational institutions, employers, etc.)

Activity Three: Discussion

1. While using pochlio in doing evaluation to the students, the teachers may encounter some problems. The following list some of the problems. Can you think of more? Discuss in a group and find more problems and also find the solutions correspondingly.

◉ Do the contents put in the pochlio need to be standardized?

◉ Who has the responsibility of choosing the materials in the pochlio? The teachers? Or the students?

◉ Does the pochlio only collect the best work of the students, or including some developing work?

◉

◉

◉

2. Evaluation affects the quality and quantity of learning. Therefore, it needs to be examined in terms of both the learning processes and the outcomes of learning.

Read the following statements. Discuss the meaning and fill in the blanks with *Process evaluation* and *Product evaluation*. (The answer is hidden somewhere in this module)

- ________ refers to the reflective assessment that is an integral part of the ongoing learning process.
- ________ is summative performance testing, aimed at gauging the learner's current language competence, skills and attitudes in relevant communicative tasks and contexts.
- ________ can provide significant information to teachers about the progress of individual learners' communicative proficiency, personal development, learning skills and social skills. This helps them to plan instructional interventions.
- ________ can provide significant information to learners about how they are progressing in terms of both their communicative and process skills, helping them to take charge of their learning.

Voice from the Theory

DEFINITION:

POCHLIO— collection of artifacts accompanied by a reflective narrative that not only helps the learner to understand and extend learning, but invites the reader of the pochlio to gain insight about learning and the learner. (Porter, Cleland, 1995:154)

POCHLIO—PORTFOLIO—PORTAFOGLIO (different spellings)

Section 4 Self-evaluation Competence as Logistics English Teachers

Problem and Reflection

Activity One:

"Pochlio", a useful way in evaluation that can be used not only to the students but the teachers themselves as self-evaluation method—"teaching pochlio". The following are some of the definitions given by researchers. Read them and give your own understanding of teaching pochlio.

- "In its most basic form, a teaching portfolio is a collection of information about a teacher's practice." Portfolio should be "structured around sound professional content standards and individual schools' goals" and should contain "commentaries and explanations of... carefully selected examples of both student and teacher work" (Stronge, 1997:194).
- "A purposeful collection of any aspect of a teacher's work that tells the story of a teacher's efforts, skills, abilities, achievements, and contributions to his/her colleagues, institution, academic discipline or community." (Brown, wolfe-Quintero, 1997:28)
- My understanding of a teaching pochlio:

____

____

____

Activity Two: Reading

Read the following teaching pochlio written by Nunan (2004:225). Think of the question:" What can be included in a teaching portfolio?"

As Director of the English Center at the University of Hong Kong, as well as a practicing teacher, my motivation in developing a portfolio was somewhat different from most teachers'. While I was keen to develop a portfolio for my own professional purposes, I also wanted to encourage the teachers in my program to develop their portfolios as part of our on-going professional development. So it was important for me to show my colleagues the value I placed on portfolio development.

My major concern in sharing my portfolio with the rest of the staff was that it might be taken as a blueprint for others to follow. I didn't want this to happen because a portfolio should represent the professional persona of the teacher, and each should be unique, not only in terms of its structure and content, but also in terms of the process through which it is created. I was also a little concerned at the reaction of my colleagues to negative comments and feedback from my students, but these had to be a part of the portfolio. If they were to be omitted, if I presented a cleaned-up version of my professional self, the value of the process, as well as the document itself, would be greatly diminished.

As I began developing the portfolio, numerous questions and doubts came to mind. I have been teaching for around 27 years, and had kept student evaluations and other documentary evidence for most of those years. How far should I reach into my professional past in order to provide an account of myself? In the end I decided to restrict the portfolio largely to my current teaching post, with some selective extracts from my former position to provide some points of comparison.

The next issue concerned content. What should the portfolio look like? What should it contain? I choose a large loose-leaf binder so I could "grow" the portfolio over time. The first things that went into the binder were an outline of my teaching duties and a statement of philosophy. I felt that the statement of philosophy was central to the portfolio creation process because it provided a reference point for what was to come.

In terms of evidence, I want to include material from as many different sources as possible. As a large part of my work is concerned with curriculum and materials development, I included samples of these kinds of products. Since it is crucial to present evidence from external sources, I also compiled data provided by students and colleagues. Student data included the formal end-of-course evaluations that are conducted by an independent unit within the university, the Center for the advancement of University Teaching. I also included extracts from my students' journals. In addition, I asked my research students to do written evaluations of my style as a research supervisor.

As soon as I had begun to assemble the various bits of evidence of myself as a teacher, I was confronted with another imperative: What was I to do with the stuff that was negative, or, if not negative, that showed a person I barely recognized, and, in some cases, didn't particularly like? Data from several of my classes showed that I needed to pay closer attention to the area of evaluation, particularly when it came to making the grading criteria explicit. Point taken. I'll work on this aspect of my teaching next semester. In another instance, the graduate students taking my course in curriculum design said they want more input from me. In other words, they want to be lectured at. This suggestion I plan to resist. With these students, the most effective learning takes place when they're productively engaged in small-group tasks. I decided to add commentary on the student evaluations in which I present my interpretation of the data along with my response to it. I work hard (although not always entirely successfully) at avoiding self-justification. Ideally, I should show the students my commentary and get their reaction to it. Unfortunately, they are now beyond my grasp.

Creating a portfolio is an enormous undertaking. I do a little each day, and by the end of the term I have a substantial document. My professional self! Or is it just one of the many professional personas that I draw on each day? My sense of satisfaction evaporates as I realize that the portfolio is never complete, that, although it is the end of semester and I can pause to draw breath professionally, this thing will grow beside me as long as I teach.

Post-reading task:

Write down your answers to the following question.

What can be included in a teaching portfolio?
1.
2.
3.
4.

(Answer:)

Standardized testing	Authentic assessment
1. Testing and instruction are regarded as separate activities	1. Assessment is an integral part of instruction
2. Students are treated in a uniform way	2. Each learner is treated as a unique person
3. Decisions are based on single sets of data(test scores)	3. Provides multiple sources of data, a more informative view
4. Emphasis on weakness / failures: what students cannot do	4. Emphasis on strengths/progress: what learners can do
5. One-shot exams	5. Ongoing assessment
6. Cultural/social-economic status bias	6. More culture-fair
7. Focus on one 'right answer'	7. Possibility of several perspectives
8. Judgement without suggestions for improvement	8. Useful information for improving / guiding learning
9. Pressures teachers to narrow teaching to what is tested	9. Allows teachers to develop meaningful curricula
10. Focus on lower-order knowledge and skills	10. Emphasis on higher-order learning outcomes and thinking skills
11. Forbids students to interact; promotes comparisons between students (norm-referencing)	11. Encourages collaborative learning; compares learners to their own past performances and the aims
12. Extrinsic learning for a grade	12. Intrinsic learning for its own sake

(Answer:)

- Process evaluation
- Product evaluation
- Process evaluation
- Process evaluation

Bibliography

Brown, J. D. , Kate W. Q. 1997. Teacher portfolios for evaluation: A great idea or a waste of time [J]? *Language Teacher* 21(1): 28-30.

Hart, D. 1994. *Authentic assessment: a handbook for educators* [M]. New York: Addison Weslwy.

Johnson, K. , Johnson, H. 1999. *Encyclopedic Dictionary of Applied Linguistics: A Handbook for Language Teaching* [M]. Blackwell Publishers Ltd.

O'Malley, M. and Price, L. V. 1996. *Authentic Assessment for English Language Learners* [M]. New York: Addison Wesley.

Porter, C. , and Janell Cleland. 1995. *The portfolio as a learning strategy* [M]. Portsmouth, NH: Boynton/Cook Publishers.

Stronge, J. . H. (ed.). 1997. *Evaluating teaching: A guide to current thinking and best practice* [M]. Thousand Oaks, CA: Corwin Press.

Wallace, M. J. 1992. *Training Foreign Language Teachers* [M]. Cambridge: Cambridge University Press.

Wood, R. 1993. *Assessment and Testing: A Survey of Research* [M]. Cambridge: Cambridge University Press.

Module Six

Competence of Applying CALL in Logistics English Teaching

Discussion:

◇ What is the basic background knowledge to CALL for logistics English teachers?

◇ What are the changing roles of teachers?

◇ What are the CALL activities for logistics English teachers?

Section 1 Logistics English Teacher's Background Knowledge to CALL

Problem and Reflection

Activity One: Fill in the activity card

1. What are the behaviouristic, communicative and integrative approaches in language learning?

2. What activities do language teachers use under the different approaches?

Activity Two: Reading

The following is anessay from COMPUTERS AND LANGUAGE LEARNING: AN OVERVIEW(Warschauer, M. & Healey, D., 1998). Read it first and do the following exercises.

The History of Call

Computers have been used for language teaching since the 1960s. This 30+ year history can be roughly divided into three main stages: behaviouristic CALL, communicative CALL, and integrative CALL. Each stage corresponds to a certain level of technology as well as a certain pedagogical approach.

Behaviouristic CALL, conceived in the 1950s and implemented in the 1960s and 1970s, could be considered a sub-component of the broader field of computer-assisted instruction. Informed by thebehaviourist learning model, this mode of CALL featured repetitive language drills, referred to as drill-and-practice (or, pejoratively, as 'drill-and-kill'). In this paradigm, especially popular in the United States, the computer was viewed as a mechanical tutor which never grew tired or judgmental and allowed students to work at an individual pace. Though behaviourist CALL eventually gravitated to the personal computer, it was first designed and implemented in the era of the mainframe. The best-known tutorial system, PLATO, ran on its own special hardware consisting of a central computer and terminals and featured extensive drills, grammatical explanations, and translation tests at various intervals (Ahmad, Corbett, Rogers, & Sussex, 1985).

The next stage, communicative CALL, emerged in the late 1970s and early 1980s, at the same time that behavioristic approaches to language teaching were being rejected at both the theoretical and pedagogical level, and when new personal computers were creating greater possibilities for individual work. Proponents of communicative CALL stressed that computer-based activities should focus more on using forms than on the forms themselves, teach grammar implicitly rather than explicitly, allow and encourage students to generate original utterances rather than just manipulate prefabricated language, and use the target language predominantly or even exclusively (Jones & fortescue, 1987; Philips, 1987; Underwood, 1984). Communicative CALL corresponded to cognitive theories which stressed that learning was a process of discovery, expression, and development. Popular CALL software developed in this period included text reconstruction programs (which allowed students working alone or in groups to rearrange words and texts to discover patterns of language and meaning) and simulations (which stimulated discussion and discovery among students working in pairs or groups). For many proponents of communicative CALL, the focus was not so much on what students did with the machine, but rather what they with each other while working at the computer.

Though communicative CALL was seen as an advance behaviouristic CALL, it too began to come under criticism. By the late 1980s and early 1990s, critics pointed out that the computer was still being used in an *ad hoc* and disconnected fashion and thus 'finds itself making a greater contribution to marginal rather than central elements' of the language learning process (Kenning & Kenning, 1990:90). This corresponded to a broader reassessment of communicative language teaching theory and practice. Many teachers were moving away from a cognitive view of communicative teaching to a more social or socio-cognitive view, which placed greater emphasis on language use in authentic social context. Task-based, project-based, and content-based approaches all sought to integrate learners in authentic environments, and also to integrate the various skills of language learning and use. This led to a new perspective on technology and language learning, which has been termed integrative CALL (Warschauer, 1996b), a perspective which seeks both to integrate various skills (e. g., listening, speaking, reading, and writing) and also integrate technology more fully into the language learning process. In integrative approaches, students learn to use a variety of technological tools as an ongoing process of language learning and use, rather than visiting the computer lab on a once a week basis for isolated exercises (whether the exercises be behaviouristic or communicative).

If the mainframe was the technology of behaviouristicCALL, and the PC the technology of communicative CALL, the multimedia-networked computer is the technology of integrative CALL. The multimedia networked computer-with a range of informational, communicative, and publishing tools now potentially at the fingertips of every student-provides not only the possibilities for much more integrated uses of technology, but also the imperative for such use, as learning to read, write, and communicate via computer has become an essential feature of modern life in the developed world.

Many of the changes in CALL paradigms flow from economic and social changes. The shift to global information-based economies has meant a dramatic increase in the need to deal with large amounts of information and to communicate across languages and cultures. Memorisation is less important in this information-rich time than effective search strategies, and students need the ability to respond and adapt to changes rather than training in a single way to approach a task. Teacher roles have also changed with the times, Teachers are rarely the sole source of language information in these days of global interconnectedness, and the literary corpus that may have been the basis of their foreign language training is not the only body of knowledge worth learning. The assumption from cognitive theory is that teachers do not pour information from their store into the heads of waiting and willing students, but that students actively interpret and organise the information they are given, fitting it into prior knowledge or revising prior knowledge in the light of what they have learned (Dole *et al.*, 1991; Van Dijk & Kintsch, 1983).

As a result of all these changes, the teacher has become a facilitator of learning rather than the font of wisdom, and will find, select, and offer information in a variety of ways on the basis of what the students must learn in order to meet diverse needs.

Having and manipulating language data in multiple media provides learners with the raw material they can use to re-create the language for themselves, using their own organising schemes. Activities that encourage students to explore and be creators of language rather than passive recipients of it further the idea of the learner as an active participant in learning (Brown, 1991). While both teachers and learners see some utility in basic language drills, such as of irregular verb forms, repetitive practice only fits into a small part of language learning when the goal is communication in the target language.

As facilitators, teachers must in many ways know more than they would as directive givers of information. Facilitators must be aware of a variety of material available for improving students' language skill, not just one or two texts. They also need to know how to teach learners to use the material effectively. Teachers as facilitators have to be able to respond to the needs that students have, not just what has been set up ahead of time based on a curriculum developer's idea of who will be in the classroom. Teacher training is a key element to success in this more flexible language classroom, so that teachers can use multimedia and other resources effectively.

Post-reading task:

Please state the three stages of the development of CALL and the characteristics of each one comparing with the related approach in language learning.

Activity Three:

1. Read the following article "Professional Development in Technology Use" (cited from Egbert et al., 2002) with the question "What is the relationship between CALL and professional development?"

Little empirical research has been conducted on computer-using language teachers' professional development. Grau's (1996) participants noted that it was hard to continue learning about technologies because the school had no resources to help teachers do so. This may be the case for many language teachers. Studies have found, though, that "teachers who spent more time in professional development activities were generally more likely... to indicate they felt well prepared" to teach with technology. Although CALL professional development materials and resources in the form of books, Web sites, electronic discussion lists, journals, and courses exists, it is unclear which of these provide the most effective development and which provide theories and activities that directly transfer to classroom implementation. We may take a cue from the Apple's "Classroom of Tomorrow" project (reported in Sandholtz, Ringstaff, & Dwyer, 1997), where hands-on, active learning by teachers allowed exploration, experimentation, and most important, reflection; these "situated teacher development" activities, in turn, supported many different kinds of change in classrooms.

2. State the reasons for supporting (or denying) the inclusion of CALL as one required competence for English language teacher's professional development.

Voice from the Theory

✖ CALL: an abbreviation for =COMPUTER ASSISTED LANGUAGE LEARNING

Section 2 The Change of the Teacher's Role in English Teaching

Problem and Reflection

Activity One: Interview

Step 1: Interview as many English teachers with the question: "What are the roles of teachers in traditional English teaching?" Add more options to the list.

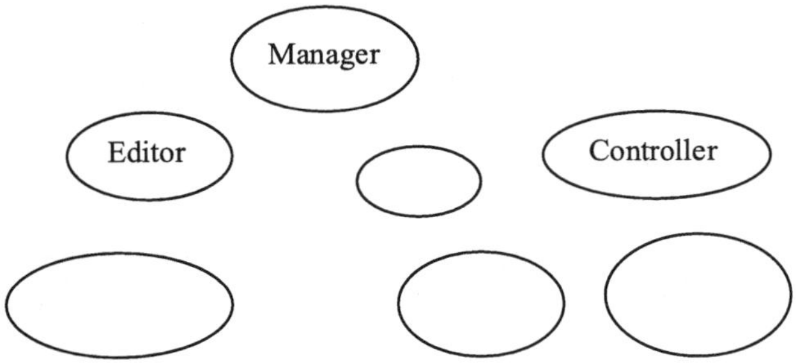

Step 2: The English teaching profession needs its own IT professionals. We increasingly need qualified language teachers who at the same time are highly skilled in the relevant aspects of IT. Considering the roles of English language teachers in CALL, with the help of the following reading article (Amiri, 2000), add more roles of the English language teachers to the above list besides the traditional roles.

Putting teachers in the driving seat

It seems that although more and more experienced teachers do use computers for word processing or running other types of commercial programs, including CALL programs and CD-ROMs, this does not give them the necessary confidence when it comes to using computers because they still do not feel in control of the machine itself. It is difficult, I believe, to have a sense of control over computers without being able to program them in some way, in the same way that it would be difficult to have a sense of control over cars without being able to drive one. One could, of course, use a car without driving it; it could be driven by someone else, a professional driver perhaps. In this case one still does go from A to B, but this is not really having control over car. Now, there are different degrees of control and different types of cars. Not many of us can drive Formula One car the way a professional Formula One racing driver such as Damon Hill or Michael Schumacher can. No one however, argues for leaving driving to professional drivers, who know more about cars , are more technically and mechanically minded, and can drive faster and better, etc. Most of us learn to drive and use that skill to meet our everyday needs. We still use public transport when necessary. The car, however, gives us the flexibility we increasingly need. Driving is perhaps a good example of a skill that despite its complexity, need for intensive training, and even risk to people's lives, has become recognised as necessary for modern life. Programming too, I would like to argue, is fast becoming a necessary and useful skill to have especially for educators.

Activity Two: Reading

The following literature is about the English language teacher's attitudes and behaviors towards IT. Comparing with yours. (Revised from Egbert et al., 2002).

Research in teacher technology use shows that preservice teachers gain confidence in the use of computer technologies through formal teacher-education coursework and that their attitudes towards computers improve through such coursework (Lam, 2000). Although this research shows changes in perceptions that are often correlated with classroom technology use, it does not explain what preservice teachers take away from the courses and actually use in their classrooms. Galloway (1996) stresses the need for research that addresses questions about what computer experience teachers need to gain, how they actually use computers, and how they learn to use and adopt computers. The literature to date that attempts to answer such questions suggests two overarching themes: first, that teachers learn what they actually need to use; and second, coursework does not always address teachers' or students' needs.

McMeniman and Evans (1998) conclude that language teachers alter their practices and beliefs when "presented with evidence that shows positive effects of the new teaching method on quality of learning outcomes" and "develop expertise in the new method". In other words, since they do not perceive that there is sufficient evidence of any positive effects of technology-enhanced teaching, many teachers may not change their practice to incorporate technology. Even when teachers do believe that technology has "empowering potential," they do not always know how to make this happen in the classroom. Wissick, Langone, and Ross (1998) also discovered that although teachers do learn new skills as a result of instruction, they do not necessarily use those skills in their daily practice or change their instructional practice in the long run.

Along the same lines, Galloway (1996) found that most teachers learned to use computers outside of coursework. While this helps to prepare teachers for CALL coursework in the use and integration of appropriate technologies, it also has other implications for teacher education in CALL. The important trend noted in both of these studies is that the majority of respondents learned to use those applications that they needed to use in their lives outside of school. Calloway explains this trend by noting that the most-used computer application among his participants was word processing. This is because teachers use word processing for both personal and professional work. Galloway also found that few teachers actually used telecommunications, hypermedia, or even other business programs such as databases and spreadsheets because they did not need to use these technologies in their lives outside of the classroom. He suggests that we show teachers how their personal and professional knowledge and experience with computers can also be used in their classroom. The United States Department of Education similarly reports that teachers use technology most frequently to prepare or supplement instruction rather than for instructional delivery, thereby working to save themselves time or to enhance student learning beyond the classroom.

Currently, what teachers are learning in coursework might not be what they need to know. Abdal-Haqq (1995) argues that teachers are not integrating new and advanced technologies into their syllabi, possibly because teacher education in computers often focuses on "older and simpler instructional applications of computer technology" rather than multimedia, problem-solving applications, and other newer tools. In short, teachers cannot implement what they do not know about. Findings indicate that even more experienced teachers use the computer mainly for word processing, spreadsheets, drills, and to some extent Internet research and problem-solving. Teachers are more likely to use these programs for creating technology in ways that fit their current practice, rather than transforming their practice through the use of technology.

Activity Three:

A wide range of factors have been found to promote and inhibit the teachers' use of computers. Examine the following factors and select the ones that influence you and your colleagues most:

The influential factors	Tick"◎"
Success in using computers	
Whether the technology is useful for job performance	
How easy it is to use	
The current use of the technology in the school	
Having a computer at home	
Time pressures both outside and during class	
Lack of resources and materials	
Insufficient or inflexible guidelines, standards, and curricula	
Lack of support or recognition for integrating computers	
Inadequate training and technical support	
Attitudes towards technology	

Section 3 CALL Activities

Problem and Reflection

Activity One:

What kinds of activities the logistics English teachers can use relating to the computer in their classroom teaching? What are your opinions of the activities?

–
–
–
–
–
–
–

Activity Two: Specification

The following is a list of the CALL activities in use. The left line is the general CALL activities provided. Supplement the right line with the designing of the specified activities in logistics English teaching.

CALL activity	Specified activities in logistics English teaching
Creating an external document	
E-mail mystery activity	
Presenting software to the class	
Using content based software	
Creating a web address book	
Participating in a professional listserv	
Creating a WebQuest	
Creating an instructional Web page for students or teachers	
Creating a personal Web page	
Developing computer enhanced lesson plans	
Reviewing software/Web sites	
Developing a technology solution for an inquiry project	
Using an electronic conferencing system	
Web portfolios	
Internet research	
Word processing	
Skill-building activities	

Activity Three: Discussion

The following is an article about" The World Wide Web". With the information getting from it, discuss with your partner:

1. What is the function of the World Wide Web in logistics English teaching?
2. What activities do logistics English teachers often use for their teaching?
3. Do you often use any of the activities?

The most recent medium of computer-mediated communication used in the second language classroom is the World Wide Web. Part library, part publishing house, part telephone, part interactive television, the Web represent one of the most diverse and revolutionary media in human history. It is already starting to transform academia, business, and entertainment; there seems little doubt that it will eventually have a profound impact on education as well.

The World Wide Web can be used in a myriad of ways for language teaching. Published accounts have discussed the use of the Web for providing linguistic exercises (e. g., Li 1995), for accessing authentic reading materials (e. g., Lixnl-Purcell, 1995), for stimulating communicative exercises such as student discussion of trip or vacations (Rosen, 1995). Because of the relative newness of the Web, as well as the difficulty in investigating use of such a broad and complex medium, relatively little research has been conducted. An exception is an ethnographic study by Warschauer (1997), who examined the uses of the Web by four language and writing classes over the course of two years. Students in all four classes published their writings and multimedia document on the World Wide Web. The study found that the impact of the Web-based word rested in large part on the social and cultural relevance of the writing assignments. When students perceived they were contributing something of value to the public arena, they put in a great deal of effort in the process and attention to the product, yielding positive results in heir learning to write in a second language. When students did not see their work as having any particular social or cultural relevance, they showed little interest in Web-based publishing and the medium itself lent little extra legitimacy or authenticity to their writing assignments.

Section 4 Other Issues in CALL

Problem and Reflection

Activity One: Fill in the activity card

1. What kind of information do you commonly obtain from Internet relating to logistics English teaching?

2. What programs do you prefer to use in the logistics English teaching?

3. What do you usually do on Internet for logistics English teaching?

Read the following article on "synchronous communication" and examine your own way of administrating it.

Synchronous or real time communication can be accomplished either using special software programs for local area networks, such as Daedalus Interchange by Daedalus Inc. or CommonSpace by Sixth Floor Media, or via the Internet, using a variety of chat media such as MOOs (technically "Multi-user domains Object Oriented"), Internet Relay Chat, or web chat programs.

Computer assisted discussion over local area networks has been especially popular in the United States, in foreign language, ESL, and English composition classes. During synchronous computer assisted discussion, each student sits at an individual computer. With program such as Daedalus Interchange, the screen is divided into two parts. Students compose their message on the bottom half of the screen. After the students hit the send button, the message appears almost instantly on the top half of all the other computers in the class. The messages are listed in chronological order, with easy scrolling for re-examining previous messages. Such discussion can be carried out among the whole class or among smaller specialized conferences.

Research on the use of computer-assisted discussion for language teaching has focused on the questions of participation, language use, and writing improvement. Numerous studies have found that computer-assisted discussion features participation which is dramatically more balanced than face-to-face discussion, with far less domination either by the teacher or by particularly vocal students. This is likely due to the fact that everyone can 'speak' at once, without having to seize the floor.

The language used in computer-assisted discussion has been shown to be more lexically and syntactically complex than in face-to-face discussion (Warschauer, 1996a). This is likely due to the written nature of computer-mediated communication, which allows more planning time than oral communication and adopts more written syntactical features. For whatever reasons, computer-mediated discussion seems to be a good vehicle for helping students push their language to greater levels of complexity. Printed transcripts of computer-mediated discussions can also be used later for grammatical analysis or lessons. Finally, there has been at least one study that claims that semester long participation in computer-assisted discussion was more beneficial to the development of students writing than was participation in oral discussion (Sullivan & Pratt, 1996).

For these reasons, many teachers of general language classes have found computer-assisted discussion advantageous on an occasional basis as a supplement to oral discussion. Writing teachers have used it on a more frequent basis, even daily.

Synchronous communication at a distance can be carried out via MOOs, Internet Relay Chat, or Web-based chat programs. MOOs have been the most popular to date, but they will likely be supplanted by web-based chatting in the future. The particular interfaces of these programs tend to result in shorter, simpler sentences than does Daedalus Interchange, which allows user to easily write longer sentences or paragraphs.

MOOs and chat seem most beneficial either when there is a particular need for long distance partners to communicate or as an out – of – class activity to give students additional time on task (Pinton, 1996).

Activity Two: Reading

1. Pre–reading questions:

- Do you often write emails to your friends in English?

Asynchronous communication is carried out most frequently via e–mail; other tools include bulletin boards, newsgroup (such as on ' USENET '), and web – based conferencing system. E – mail is most direct in that messages go directly to students' individual mailboxes. The other systems, which require students to log on to sites to read messages, lack the convenience of e–mail; they do, however, allow messages to be threaded, thus, facilitating more easy access to particular parts of long, complex discussions among many people.

E–mail and other forms of asynchronous computer–mediated communication have been used for a variety of purposes in second language classes. Many teachers in college and university writing classes have used e–mail discussion groups within their classes to give students opportunities for authentic writing assignments (see, for example, a series of article by Janda in Warschauer, 1995). Teachers at all levels, from primary to tertiary, have used long – distance e – mail exchanges to give students greater opportunities for authentic communication (either with native speakers or with other learners of the language). And for carrying out collaborative projects, such as comparison of film and literature (Soh & Soon, 1991), compilations of folklore (Gaer, 1995). Business simulations (Feldman, 1995), and survey–based research (Kendall, 1995).

Research the uses of e–mail in the language classroom is complicated by the fact that much of the communication takes place outside class hours and in uncontrolled conditions. At least two ethnographic studies have attempted to describe the processes and results of using e–mail over the period of a semester. Tella (1991; 1992a; 1992b) followed several Finnish high school classes as they carried out an exchange with classrooms in England. He found that, compared to the ordinary English classes in Finland, these classes became much more learner-centered, with learners' time and effort devoted to authentic reading and writing tasks related to the authentic communication with partners in England. Warschauer (1997) looked at the use of e-mail between a teacher and her students in a graduate ESL writing class; he found that e-mail was a powerful medium for apprenticeship learning, with the teacher able to provide students with detailed and rapid feedback on the immediate problems and questions that they had. This benefit, though, seemed largely due to the teachers' willingness to put a lot of time and effort into reading and responding to students' e-mail message, a luxury that many teachers might not have. Finally, a study by Wang (1993) compared dialogue journals written with paper and pencil (by one group of ESL students) and transmitted over e-mail (by a second group). She found that the e-mail group communicated more frequently, asked more questions, responded to more questions, and used a greater variety of language functions than did the paper-and-pencil group.

2. The following article "THE BORDERLESS WORLD?" (Hanna, 2003) is about electronic discussion. Read it to find the ways in which electronic discussion inflects and is inflected by cultural and generic expectations.

Language learning provides fertile ground for the co-existence of two contradictory views of Internet use. On the one hand, there is the idea of the borderless world where the Internet flattens out cultural difference. On the other hand, we continue to assert the existence of virtual boundaries: While the physical borders may be irrelevant, the Internet is the superhighway into the heart of another culture, giving instant access to difference. When we send off our students via modem to practice their French in an electronic discussion forum, the contradiction gets played out as follows: We have deceptively easy access to our linguistic and cultural other, but this other is assumed to be doing the same thing as we are only in French. The ways in which electronic discussion may be inflected by cultural and generic expectations risk being ignored.

We have reason to be suspicious of the assumption of the flattening out of cultural difference. Although Internet fora notionally transcend national and cultural boundaries, as soon as communication occurs, cultural practices are necessarily activated. Thus, while participants in a given discussion list view it as a forum for debate, their notions of what constitutes acceptable forms of debate may differ according to cultural affiliations. Wider cultural patterns in rhetorical ploys, explicitness of communication, use of irony and humor, repertoires of textual features available for pastiche, as well as strategies for engaging in cross-cultural communication will come into play. In this way, French participants are likely to apply expectations regarding other forms of intellectual debate. However these wider cultural patterns are necessarily adapted to this particular cultural practice or genre—electronic discussion—a genre with its own technical constraints (length, speed of reply, formatting) and discursive/rhetorical conventions. These conventions may vary culturally but also from site to site (subculturally).

We may therefore assume that any electronic discussion group potentially brings together participants with divergent expectations of what appropriate behavior in a site of public discussion might be. It follows that in order to ensure the continued functioning of the group, mechanisms exist for dealing with such inter-cultural (or inter-subcultural) differences. The most visible of these weshall call "moderation". This term commonly denotes intervention by an official moderator to deal with unsuitable messages; however, commentary by other participants on the appropriateness of contributions may fulfill a very similar function. In such cases, the official moderator is not alone in monitoring the list, initiating new members, or attempting to exclude inappropriate behavior, and for this reason we shall use the term moderation broadly to cover official and unofficial intervention.

Through both of these forms of moderation, questions regarding suitability are raised and dealt with at regular intervals, and various justifications are offered for treating contributions as acceptable or otherwise. In a forum where this policing of appropriate behavior is carried out with a minimum of congeniality, moderation can function as a kind of initiation or indeed informal teaching. In this way, the Internet discussion forum offers a potentially privileged site for students to get individual feedback on their performance from people other than the teacher.

Activity Three: Discussion

Google (www. Google. com) has been proved to be an effective searching engine for its quick and powerful function. Discuss and get peer-support about the direction of the following aspects of Google and the following useful web sites:

- ▶ Basic searching method
- ▶ Searching for images
- ▶ Searching for directory
- ▶ Explanation for English vocabulary
- ▶ Filtering
- ▶ Calculator

◇ The useful web sites in logistics and supply chain management:

http://www. logisticsworld. com/

http://www. inboundlogistics. com

http://www. careersinsupplychain. org/

◇ The useful web sites in foreign language teaching and learning:

http://calico. cog (CALICO journal)

http://www. iste. org/publish/caell. html (CAELL journal)

http://www. swets. nl/sps/journals/call. html (CALL)

http://www. aitech. ac. jp (Internet TESL journal)

http://polyglot. cal. msu. edu (Language Learning & Technology)

http://www. cltr. uq. oz. au:8000/oncall/ochome. htm (On-CALL)

http://www-writing. berkeley. edu (TESL-EJ)

http://www. tesol. edu (TESOL CALL Interest Section)

Bibliography

Amiri, F. 2000. IT-literacy for language teachers: should it include computer programming? [J] *System*, 28(1), 77-84.

Egbert, J., Paulus, T. M., Nakamichi, Y. 2002. The impact of CALL instruction on classroom computer use: A foundation for rethinking technology in teacher education [J]. *Language Learning & Technology*, 6(3), 108-126.

Hanna, B. E., & de Nooy, J. 2003. A funny thing happened on the way to the forum: Electronic discussions and foreign language learning[J]. *Language Learning & Technology*, 7(1), 71-85.

Johnson, K., Johnson, H. 1999. *Encyclopedic Dictionary of Applied Linguistics: A Handbook for Language Teaching* [M]. Blackwell Publishers Ltd.

Warschauer, M. & Healey, D. 1998. Computers and language learning: An overview [J]. *Language Teaching*, 31,57-71.

Module Seven

Collaborative Competence of Logistics English Teachers

Discussion:

◇ How do you understand communities of practice?

◇ How to design collaborative activities in logistics English teaching?

Section 1 Understanding Communities of Practice

Problem and Reflection

Activity One: Fill in the activity card

1. Do you prefer to work alone or work in groups to solve the problems in logistics English teaching?

2. What are the benefits of working in groups?

Activity Two: Reading

What are communities of practice?

Communities of practice are formed by people who engage in a process of collective learning in a shared domain of human endeavor: a tribe learning to survive, a band of artists seeking new forms of expression, a group of engineers working on similar problems, a clique of pupils defining their identity in the school, a network of surgeons exploring novel techniques, a gathering of first-time managers helping each other cope. In a nutshell:

Communities of practice are groups of people who share a concern or a passion for something they do and learn how to do it better as they interact regularly.

Note that this definition allows for, but does not assume, intentionality: learning can be the reason the community comes together or an incidental outcome of member's interactions. Not everything called acommunity is a community of practice. A neighborhood for instance, is often called a community, but is usually not a community of practice. Three characteristics are crucial:

1. *The domain*: A community of practice is not merely a club of friends or a network of connections between people. It has an identity defined by a shared domain of interest. Membership therefore implies a commitment to the domain, and therefore a shared competence that distinguishes members from other people. (You could belong to the same network as someone and never know it.) The domain is not necessarily something recognized as "expertise" outside the community. A youth gang may have developed all sorts of ways of dealing with their domain: surviving on the street and maintaining some kind of identity they can live with. They value their collective competence and learn from each other, even though few people outside the group may value or even recognize their expertise.
2. *The community*: In pursuing their interest in their domain, members engage in joint activities and discussions, help each other, and share information. They build relationships that enable them to learn from each other. A website in itself is not a community of practice. Having the same job or the same title does not make for a community of practice unless members interact and learn together. The claims processors in a large insurance company or students in American high schools may have much in common, yet unless they interact and learn together, they do not form a community of practice. But members of a community of practice do not necessarily work together on a daily basis. The impressionists, for instance, used to meet in cafes and studios to discuss the style of painting they were inventing together. These interactions were essential to making them a community of practice even though they often painted alone.
3. *The practice*: A community of practice is not merely a community of interest—people who like certain kinds of movies, for instance. Members of a community

of practice are practitioners. They develop a shared repertoire of resources: experiences, stories, tools, ways of addressing recurring problems—in short a shared practice. This takes time and sustained interaction. A good conversation with a stranger on an airplane may give you all sorts of interesting insights, but it does not in itself make for a community of practice. The development of a shared practice may be more or less self-conscious. The "windshield wipers" engineers at an auto manufacturer make a concerted effort to collect and document the tricks and lessons they have learned into a knowledge base. By contrast, nurses who meet regularly for lunch in a hospital cafeteria may not realize that their lunch discussions are one of their main sources of knowledge about how to care for patients. Still, in the course of all these conversations, they have developed a set of stories and cases that have become a shared repertoire for their practice.

It is the combination of these three elements that constitutes a community of practice. And it is by developing these three elements in parallel that one cultivates such a community. (Wenger, 2006)

Activity Two: Reading

The following is a discussion about collaborative teaching held in three teachers, try to join them. (http://educationforum.ipbhost.com/index.php? showtopic=3289)

"I not only use all of the brains I have, but all I can borrow.": The uses of ICT for collaborative teaching and learning.

The main point of my presentation is to recommend the elements that should be integrated into the proposed E-HELP website to make it the most collaborative environment possible. Before I do so, I intend to discuss the reasons why collaboration is a good idea in the first place, along with potential barriers and methods of doing so.

1. Reasons for collaboration

One of the main reasons for collaboration in teaching is the widening of horizons that it brings. The reason we teach is so that pupils learn: the more we know and the better we can deliver it, the more pupils are likely to learn. As with any job, you take into the workplace your own 'toolkit' of skills and ideas. Collaboration is one of the best ways to add to this toolkit and therefore do your best for the pupils in your charge. With collaboration, of course, comes 'networking' - getting to know and trust others who share similar interests. In turn, there are opportunities for both professional development and career advancement.

It's all very well being 'trained' en masse by a representative of the company which is supplying your new interactive whiteboard. A one-to-one demonstration by a colleague is much better. It is this peer-learning which is an intrinsic part of collaboration: knowledge and skills are cascaded throughout the community by willing volunteers. At the end of the day, collaboration can be summed by being good practice-as Aristotle would have said, it is a good, an end-in-itself. Or as Alexander Solzehnitsyn rather succinctly put it: "Talent is always conscious of its own abundance, and does not object to sharing."

2. Barriers to collaboration

I'm sure we've all experienced the situation where at a meeting everyone within the department has agreed that resources should be shared. What happens in practice is that the more conscientious members of the department keep adding to the pool of resources, whilst others simply take them without giving back. A 'why should I?' attitude then prevails-the sharer becomes disillusioned as they realise they are perhaps the only one putting in the extra work. The non-sharers notice the shift in opinions and think, "well if she's not bothering, why should I?"

Of course, many teachers are reluctant to share their resources not out of selfishness but out of a sense of insecurity. It is often the case that, with a lack of feedback through informal observations, etc., teachers are often unaware as to how good the materials they produce actually are. Coupled to this is the presumption that to share something it must not only be good but that it must be complete. Given that different teachers use resources in a variety of ways this is nonsense. Something half-finished can be as good, if not better than something presented in toto. Each teacher puts a different slant on what they teach. A resource-for example a Powerpoint presentation on the causes of World War I-may be used as an introduction to the topic by one teacher.

Another teacher it has been shared with may tinker with it to use it as a revision tool. There is no need for shared resources to be complete, but if they are they must be editable.

Collaboration also breeds flexibility. Imagine you've planned a lesson for tomorrow on interpretations regarding the execution of Charles I. You convert relevant videos to digital files and then chop them up into relevant sections. The lesson is planned: you are going to focus on how the execution is portrayed in the film 'Cromwell' as opposed to 'To Kill a King'. As you're packing up for the day a colleague drops in for a chat. During the conversation he mentions how much his pupils enjoyed watching the Blackadder version of Charles' execution. He lends you a copy of it, you incorporate it into your lesson the following day, and not only does it add an extra dimension to your lesson but the pupils remember it and the fun they had in History. Collaboration is as much about off-the-cuff suggestions and informal ideas as it is about sharing complete and finished resources.

Sadly, there are some teachers-hopefully not many-for whom such collaboration is seen as a threat. As one of the non-sharers in the example above, the threatened teacher sees sharing and collaboration as a dilution of talent rather than an opportunity to enhance pupil learning. They see a certain resource or style of teaching as being 'theirs', meaning that anyone else either cannot do as good a job, or is somehow 'stealing' something of theirs. These teachers have to be shown that the bigger the pool of resources and ideas, the better! Intellectual property is a myth.

There is one thing which I must take issue with regarding collaboration. Some teachers feel that if they share resources their name must be plastered all over it so that they receive due recognition. As Brian Tracy, the management guru, once wrote, "the more credit you give away, the more will come back to you." If the aim is the development of pupil understanding and knowledge, why must the person who put together the resource attempt to turn themselves into a minor celebrity? I have heard some argue that it makes pupils aware that their teacher is in touch with others who share both resources and good practice. Seeing as the majority of pupils half-believe that I live in the History Office at our school, I find this hard to swallow. As Edgar Quinet stated, "what we share with another ceases to be our own." It's better than being your own–it now belongs to the community of which you are a part!

So much for reluctant sharers. Imagine that we are now dealing with an individual who recognizes the benefits of collaboration and is looking to share with teachers other than those in her department. She turns to the Internet but runs into a problem: in order to share resources and ideas, our potential sharer must get to grips with both technology and ICT jargon. There is a crucial moment, a delicate balance, in all this. As sharing over the Internet is a purely voluntary exercise, if it becomes too difficult or time-consuming then the potential collaborator is put off–perhaps never to try again. Even if she is successful in 'posting' something on the Internet, there is no guarantee that she will be either correctly understood or interpreted. It is crucial that the E-HELP website addresses these issues through necessary guides and explanations.

3. Methods of collaboration

Communities only exist in terms of relationships between their members. To build a virtual community requires a structured way of allowing relations to develop, and one of the best ways of doing this is through online discussion forums. Two of the most successful I have come across to do with education are The Education Forum and the Schoolhistory Forum. These are havens of advice, ideas and resources, mixing both formal and informal elements to create a forward-thinking, safe, and friendly atmosphere. It is the virtual equivalent of the quick chat over a cup of coffee in the faculty staff room - except that your staff room is now infinitely larger and you can 'eavesdrop' on other people's conversations by searching through previous threads! It is the little things which often make an average lesson into a great one, and such forums are repositories of small but effective ideas. The E-HELP website should certainly have an online discussion forum to add a sense of community and to make it an interactive and ever-changing destination. This will give it a great deal of user-ownership.

Discussion forums are great for linking to other websites and for describing things in words. Sometimes, however, you want a resource you can quickly adapt for a particular class. This is where resource exchanges come in–the online equivalent of photocopying each others' resources folder. A few years ago the NGFL set up the Teacher Resource

Exchange, a highly-organized and categorized place where teachers can share resources and ideas. Although unfinished resources can be uploaded and comments made upon what is shared, there is a sense of a lack of user ownership. I have tried to remedy this with the recent launch of mrbelshaw. co. uk/shareforum, which attempts to be a cross between a discussion forum and resource exchange. It is a simple concept: registered users create a new thread for each resource they wish to share, adding a short description of what it is and how it can be used. Whilst anyone can download shared files, only registered users can add comments, ask questions of the original sharer, etc. The original posting with the downloadable file will always be at the top of the thread. If the E-HELP website has a facility such as this it would be a very attractive feature.

Some may be wondering why all this is necessary - what about good old email? Well, there are advantages and disadvantages of this method. One major disadvantage, of course, is the number of people who can access what is being shared. When resources are posted on a website they are of a 'pull' nature-you can access what you want when you need it. Email, on the other hand, is 'push' oriented-you can only access what someone has sent you and you have stored somewhere. However, one major advantage of email and other one-to-one methods of collaboration (such as burning CDs/DVDs) is getting round draconian copyright legislation. (It baffles me why, as teachers, we are subject to the same rigid laws as 'pirates' who run off thousands of copies of a DVD for ill-gotten gain.) Sharing a video clip on a website it likely to get you into trouble; sharing it by email, by post or in person makes it less likely. It is for this reason that the 'personal message' (PM) functions of message boards are so useful. Things can be said and suggested which, whilst useful for teaching and learning, may fall foul of out-of-date legislation. I recommend that the E-HELP website includes such a feature.

There is a way to anonymize sharing and to get round copyright legislation, although it is only really useful at present for large files which quite a lot of people access. Peer-to-peer (P2P) technology changes the way in which users on the Internet can download files. Normally, computers download the desired file directly from the 'server' which makes the file available. Using P2P technology, however, the computer requesting the file downloads different parts of the file from different computers. Each computer is effectively turned into a 'mini-server':

The whole file does not even have to have finished downloading on one machine for it to be shared with the rest of the network. Whatever has been downloaded by one computer is shared with other computers requesting the file. So long as one full copy exists somewhere in the network, all computers will eventually receive the file! At the moment it is necessary for there to be a 'tracker' on at least one machine in the network to co-ordinate file-sharing. In the future, however, such trackers will be built into the software each computer must be running to download the file in the first place. There will be no need for a central tracker (e. g. Exeem. Of course, this will be a great boon for people who use the Internet for nefarious purposes: if there is no central tracker which can be closed down, they are a lot less likely to be caught! However, it will also be useful to the average Internet user as it will mean both greater reliability and faster downloads.

Why is P2P an important technology in terms of the E-HELP website? Well, people who host websites charge for the amount of data which is transferred from your website to other people. In other words you pay more the more successful your website is. The problem is even greater when large filesizes are involved: it only takes a relatively small number of people to download them for it to cost the site owner a lot of money. With P2P technology this problem is lessened. The more popular the file, the less likely that most users will be downloading it directly from the originating website. Although in the past setting up trackers, etc. was a job which demanded a high degree of expertise, new systems such as Blogtorrent have made the system a lot simpler. A visual interface means that users with sufficient priviledges are able to add files to the server through their browser. Users can likewise download files from a link through their web browser. In the future I envisage P2P technology being part of the normal Internet experience. The necessary client-side software will be embedded in browsers: the user will notice no difference between downloading straight from the originating website as opposed to from 'peers'. Many websites shy away from allowing large-filesize downloads for fear of cost implications. I believe that the E-HELP website should embrace P2P technology meaning that large-filesize downloads become part-and-parcel of the site.

4. The E-HELP website

I'm sure we're all aware of the difference between a lesson's content and the style of delivery. You may have the best lesson content in the world but if your delivery isn't up to much then it counts for nothing. That's one of the first lessons I learnt as a student teacher! It's the same with websites: having great content means nothing nowadays, the way it is presented is paramount. Organization is the key: a successful website has a logical structure and way of organizing its elements. Traditionally this has meant employing web design consultants to look after both what you are saying on your website and how you say it. Fortunately, there is a better way...

A Content Management System (CMS) is like the most efficient and glamorous personal assistant in the world. It categorizes any information given, making relevant links between it and other elements. Everything is presented in an organised way which is easy on the eye. Creating new content therefore is not a laborious, time-consuming and technically-demanding occupation. In fact, each user becomes a content-maker-meaning that the website itself becomes a truly collaborative effort! How much does this wonderful technology cost? Nothing! In the true spirit of collaboration, many CMS's are what is known as 'Open Source', meaning that not only are they free-of-charge but they can be modified and adapted as you see fit. The four which I would currently recommend, depending on how they are to be deployed, are Moodle, Drupal, Xoops and Mambo. Each of these can be previewed at opensourcecms. com.

Combining all I have said above into some semblance of a conclusion, I see the E-HELP website as being a place where collaborations can take place in an unstructured yet organized way. The collaborations will be unstructured in that the website will not prescribe what kinds of collaboration may take place; they will be organized, however, in that the products of such collaborations will be easily accessible and well-categorized. I envisage videos and other resources regarding good practice being made available for easy download via P2P technology. The website would also foster formal, semi-formal and informal partnerships, not least through the discussion forum. Hopefully, the CMS decided upon will allow for all of these elements to be coherently integrated so that the user can get on with collaborating rather than getting to grips with technology!

 Here's description of a very small-scale collaboration arrangement:

A few years ago the teachers of French in Kalmar district realised that they were few and far between, and that they were all re-inventing the wheel all the time. They were all using the same textbooks, and they were all part of Kalmar Council's computer network.

The problems they faced were, amongst others, that when someone was ill, the substitute often had no idea what was going on, and often wasn't even a French teachers. Another one was that when they needed to replace a textbook, the decision was often made on the loosest of grounds, because everyone was over-worked. The solution was to create a collaborative network of French teachers, where they divided a task, such as creating supplementary material for the textbook between them, and built up a bank of self-access material which all of them could draw on. It was necessary to get the copyright situation sorted out, but the 'payment' each received was really the mutual aid of their colleagues.

I haven't heard the details of the scheme for about a year, but when I last talked to anyone involved, they'd built up a bank of lesson plans for substitute teachers, and a bank of supplementary materials for the course book.

I have a strong feeling, though, that this worked because it was sufficiently small-scale for everyone involved to feel that they were benefitting directly.

 One of the main reasons for collaboration in teaching is the widening of horizons that it brings. The reason we teach is so that pupils learn: the more we know and the better we can deliver it, the more pupils are likely to learn. As with any job, you take into the workplace your own 'toolkit' of skills and ideas. Collaboration is one of the best ways to add to this toolkit and therefore do your best for the pupils in your

charge. With collaboration, of course, comes 'networking' -getting to know and trust others who share similar interests. In turn, there are opportunities for both professional development and career advancement.

When I first started teaching I was lucky to be in a history department that encouraged its members to produce and share resources. Although, as in most departments, there were some members who rarely contributed to the "resource bank".

I also shared resources with members of other departments. For example, we worked very closely with the English and Art departments when studying the First World War. This included sharing resources and ideas. It also involved arranging to teach certain topics at certain times of the academic year. For example, it made sense for the English department to study the War Poets while the history department was looking at trench warfare.

More importantly we also collaborated with local schools. In the late 1970s we had regular meetings at the local teacher centre. This gave us the opportunity of sharing resources. This was especially useful when studying local history topics. This no longer happens. Most teacher centres and LEA history advisers (who organized these meetings) are long gone.

As Doug points out, modern technology means it is now fairly easy for teachers to share resources. One you have created a free website your resources can be used by teachers and students all over the world. For example, of those who use my website, only about 35% come from the UK.

One of the great strengths of this approach is that it is fairly easy for teachers to take the material from their website and adapt it for their own use. Luckily, there are enough people in the world willing to share their resources in this way. However, these attempts at sharing have been undermined by the decision of the UK government to bring in e-learning credits. This has encouraged some teachers from providing free materials and instead they have gone over to subscription only models of delivery. This move was obviously made to please major corporations who were finding it impossible to make profits from the production of teaching materials (both online and in more conventional formats). Instead of this act of corruption, the government should have been looking for ways to encourage teachers to share resources. For example, by paying them to produce free materials.

It is not enough to rely on teachers to provide materials free of charge. We also need to create networks that enable teachers to work together on different resource producing projects. This is one of the things that E-HELP is committed to doing. The meeting in Toulouse was the first stage in achieving this objective.

Section 2 Collaborative Developing Competence

Problem and Reflection

Activity One:

In the process of teaching, the teacher might think of some questions relating to collaborative activities. Try to answer the following questions before designing any activities.

1. How do I decide which assignments/activities to make collaborative?
2. How do I divide students into groups?
3. How can I help students learn to work in groups?
4. How can I deal with conflicts within the groups?
5. How do I grade collaborative work?
6. In what ways can technology support the goals of collaborative learning?

Activity Two: Reading

The followingis an excerpt from Diane M. Enerson, R. Neill Johnson, Susannah Milner, and Kathryn M. Plank, The Penn State Teacher II: Learning to Teach, Teaching to Learn (University Park, PA: The Pennsylvania State University, 1997) on collaborative activities. Read the answers to the questions of Activity One from their own experiences.

How do I decide which assignments/activities to make collaborative? — A good rule of thumb is that if there's no reason for an activity to be collaborative, perhaps it shouldn't be. As you contemplate making a project collaborative, consider these questions: What is the objective or goal of this assignment or activity? How will that objective be furthered by asking students to work in groups? Is this project complex and challenging enough that it would be impossible for an individual student to complete it alone? Will this project require students to synthesize their work in true collaboration, rather than just complete work separately and turn it in together at the end? Collaborative activities, large or small, work best when they draw on the strengths of group interaction — for example, a rough draft workshop in a writing class allows each writer to receive comments from several different readers. In a more long – term collaborative project, such as an engineering senior design project, one of the objectives may be to teach students to draw on the skills and abilities of each member of a team. Engineering students, like students from nearly every discipline, need effective collaboration skills upon graduation if they are to enter the workplace successfully.

How do I divide students into groups? —Once you have decided to use a collaborative activity, one of the first issues you'll face is the composition of the groups. How many students should be in each group? Should you let them choose their teammates, or should you arrange the groups? Should you divide them by ability level? By demographics? To get heterogeneous groups or homogenous groups? Obviously, the answer to all of these questions depends in part on your objectives for the assignment. Group size can range anywhere from two, for an informal problem–solving session in the middle of the class period, to eight, for a semester–long team assignment. In the latter case, the group is large enough that there will probably be subgroups within the group. Karl A. Smith suggests starting out with small groups so that students become accustomed to the different roles necessary for effective groups before moving to larger groups. Of course, group size is largely determined by the amount of work the project requires—if the assignment only provides enough work for three people, a group of five will be bored, ineffective, and probably dissatisfied.

Whether or not you let students self – select their groups also depends on your purpose and the type of assignment. For short, informal in – class activities, asking students to turn to a neighbor or a friend may be the quickest and simplest way to divide the class. Even for more formal assignments, some instructors find that letting students form their own groups according to established criteria is a successful practice. Most teachers agree, however, that when you plan an extensive collaborative activity, such as a major class project, it is better for you to arrange the groups. Students who choose to work with friends often have a harder time with group projects than students in groups chosen by the teacher. Arranging the groups yourself allows you to draw on your knowledge of the abilities, interests, and needs of individuals to create increased opportunities for learning.

You can use a variety of criteria for selecting the groups. If you're teaching an upper-division course in the major, for example, where all students share the same background knowledge, you may simply want to make a random selection, or group students with similar areas of interest together. On the other hand, if the goal of the project is for groups to integrate a variety of skills, you may want to sort students so that each group has a mix of background experience, abilities, work styles, and approaches to learning. It is probably best not to group students strictly by ability level, as some diversity generally fosters increased learning among the entire group. In addition, grouping by past performance is difficult because successful collaboration requires different skills from successful individual projects; you may find that students who earn high marks on individual assignments are not the most effective group members in your class.

How can I help students learn to work in groups? — As mentioned above, your students don't necessarily know how to work in groups. After years of working independently and competitively, they may find cooperation and collaboration difficult concepts to accept in an academic setting. They are so accustomed to individual grades that it may not be obvious to them how to work together when their grade depends, in part, on the performance of other students in the class. This lack of preparation may undermine the effectiveness of your collaborative assignment and keep students from meeting the objectives of the project. For example, if each of the four students working together on a newsletter treat the project like an individual assignment rather than synthesizing their efforts, the final product will be disjointed rather than seamless.

Moreover, the students in such a group are unlikely to learn how to make effective use of the experience. To prepare them to work together as a team, you might start the group project with team-building activities such as Bob Melton's spaghetti tower, followed by a debriefing or a discussion of the group dynamics that surface during the exercise. These activities help students to recognize each other's strengths and work styles, and make them more aware of the internal resources their group might draw on for a more serious project. Any in-class group activity that requires all the members of the group to work together to achieve a common goal can be used as a starting point for a discussion of group dynamics.

In helping their students learn to work as members of a team, some teachers identify separate roles within effective groups (note-taker, agenda-setter, and so on) and ask each group to divide the roles between the members. Others administer a personality instrument like the Myers-Briggs Type Inventory, followed by a session on how each personality type translates to work styles and relationships. Karl A. Smith emphasizes the balance between positive interdependence—the idea that no student can succeed without the success of the rest of the group—and individual accountability within groups. He encourages teachers to explain these concepts and make expectations and objectives clear from the start of the project. Kris Bosworth writes that most students have the interpersonal skills that are necessary for effective group work, but that they consider these skills social rather than academic. She suggests that teachers identify these social skills and use modeling and other methods to help students bring their interpersonal experience explicitly into the classroom to promote collaborative learning. Whatever method they use to bring students together in teams, experienced teachers agree that effective collaborative activities depend on students taking individual responsibility for their work and that of the other members of their group, and using communication and teamwork skills to maintain a productive group relationship.

How can I deal with conflicts within the groups? — The first step is to realize that some conflict is perhaps inevitable—and maybe even desirable. Part of what students are learning in a group project is how to negotiate differences and deal with other people to reach a common goal.

Groups sometimes become stronger as they work through the conflicts that arise with the clash of different ideas and work habits. As Miller, Trimbur, and Wilkes point out, "excessive conflict can certainly interfere with performance. Paradoxically, excessive harmony can do the same, because members of the best groups tend to be critical of one another's work or at least to tolerate an in-house critic; they tend also to impose high standards on themselves." Of course, this kind of creative tension doesn't worry most teachers as much as the potential personality conflicts that sometimes cause bitter feelings and unproductive groups.

One of the best ways to deal with such conflicts is to prevent them from happening in the first place. As we have mentioned, some conflict arises out of the fact that students don't necessarily know how to work in groups. After years of developing individual skills in competition, students need to learn how to trust other group members, how to delegate, how to negotiate, and many other team skills. Helping students understand group dynamics can also prevent conflicts. Miller, Trimbur, and Wilkes identify personality characteristics and learning styles as two areas that shape the dynamics of the group, and encourage teachers to accommodate these differences by providing groups with ways of dealing with conflict as it arises. They argue that, although educating students about group process takes class time that might be spent on course content, spending a class period discussing group work skills can make a major difference in the success of the project. "We should teach the skills that we are grading. Thus, such a session should include a briefing on the necessity for and logistics of good communication and organization and give participants an opportunity to discuss the various kinds of talents and individual differences or preferences that different people bring to tasks." They suggest activities such as small groups solving a simple puzzle and reflecting on the group process afterward, students roleplaying, group interaction and discussing scenarios as a class, or reading and discussing information about the characteristics of different work styles and personality types, and how to accommodate these differences.

No matter how well you prepare, however, variables outside your control ensure that conflicts will sometimes occur. Keeping in touch with the progress of the groups —

through periodic progress reports or team assessments, for example—allows you to identify problems within the groups as they arise. If a group is having trouble resolving a problem, you will want to decide how active a role you are willing to take to help your students handle the situation. One strategy is to invite students to your office both individually and as a group to discuss the problem and possible approaches to a solution. During these meetings, you may find that students who are unhappy have not talked to the other members of their group about their dissatisfaction. By acting as a temporary discussion facilitator among the members of the group, you help students develop skills for dealing with confrontation and encourage them to talk with each other about the problems they are having. Sometimes, students request a change to the group membership. Most teachers experienced in collaborative approaches believe that groups should be changed only in the most extreme cases, when every other avenue for resolution has failed. When students realize that they will not be permitted to change groups easily, they feel more committed to negotiating problems within their groups. Make it clear that you expect groups to work through their differences, and they will be more likely to do so. Making changes to the groups sets the group process back to the beginning, and discards the benefits that have come from early interaction — even if some of that interaction has been confrontational.

How do I grade collaborative work? —Assessment of a collaborative activity is probably the biggest challenge teachers face when using this method. Collaborative activities often have several goals — individual learning on the part of each student, the successful functioning of a team, and a collaborative product that may be measured against diverse criteria. In other words, one reason why it is difficult to evaluate collaboration is that you must examine the process as well as the product of the group's work. Usually, long-term collaborative activities finish with a product created by all of the members of the team. In such a group project, how is individual work to be evaluated? Alternatively, the group process may end with each student turning in an individual assignment to be graded. In such cases, how can a teacher assess the success of the group? No matter what kind of project the students create, evaluation works best when it takes into account both product and process.

The most obvious thing to evaluate when grading a collaborative project is the final product. In some activities, students work as a group while projects are graded individually. For example, a group of students in a landscape architecture class might work as a group to create a design for a garden in a public space on campus. Such a project would require the team to research the public's needs, the existing vegetation, and the feasibility for changes within a certain budget and time frame. The final product would include a design for the garden and a document addressing the issues researched by the students. One way to grade this project on an individual basis would be for the group to divide the work into identifiable sections and for each member to be responsible for one section. For instance, one student would research the possibilities and limitations of the space, another would write the report, and yet another would draw the design. Instead of grading the project as a unified whole, the teacher would evaluate each section and assign individual grades to each student. This type of project can have some drawbacks, as the final product may be disjointed and uneven, and the teacher may find it difficult to evaluate each individual part for a separate grade — particularly if some students were responsible only for research rather than for writing or drawing. Another way to assign individual grades to a final product would be for the students to work as a group in the researching and planning stages, with each student then turning in his or her own design for the garden. The group would function as a common resource as the students worked on their designs, but each student would be graded on an individual "final product."

However, most long-term collaborative projects finish with each group turning in one document, design, or model that represents the collective work of the entire group — and is graded as such. In the example above, group members would work together at each level of the assignment, researching and writing together, and the final design and document would represent the work of a team rather than a group of individual workers. The teacher would then grade the design and the document as a single product, assigning the same grade for the final product to each member of the team — although individual grades might change when each student's contribution to the group process is taken into account. This type of project tends to capture the ideal of collaboration more effectively than individually graded projects, because each member of the team feels responsible for every part of the assignment. Whether the group's product is evaluated on an individual or a collective basis, however, a collaborative project is much more than the final document. Usually, one basic objective for such a project is that students learn to work as team members. How can you measure whether each student has achieved this objective? As anyone who has ever worked on a group project realizes, a successful final product does not necessarily mean that the group functioned as a team and that each member contributed equally to the work. In response to this characteristic of groups, teachers who employ collaborative activities have created several methods of evaluating group process and determining whether each student demonstrated personal accountability for the project. As is true with all other teaching methods, the best results will generally be obtained by using multiple assessments throughout the project, rather than focusing only on a single evaluation at the end.

One way of assessing the effectiveness of the groups is to monitor and observe the members' interactions as they work together. Observation gives you an understanding of the quality of each group's interaction and their progress on the assignment. This kind of observation can take place in the classroom, if groups are working together in class, or through group progress reports and updates turned in during the project. When observing in class, you can look for signs of productive group work — attentive listening, serious discussion, and progress toward a shared goal with input from each member of the group. Another informal way some teachers observe their students in collaboration is by having the teams use e-mail to communicate progress, plans and decisions as they conduct their project, and by asking students to send copies of these procedural messages to the teacher's e-mail address. This allows the teacher to observe unobtrusively the interaction of the group. Finally, some teachers use periodical progress reports to monitor their groups. When they read the reports, they check that the group is following a work plan and making progress together toward a specific goal. Progress reports are useful because they encourage students to reflect on the effectiveness of their group throughout the project, and to articulate plans for completing the assignment. For example, many teachers ask their students to complete weekly progress reports describing the tasks that each group member has completed, outlining the tasks to be completed in the next week, and confidentially commenting on each group member's contributions. Two or three required progress reports turned in during a long term group project can help you assess how well groups are achieving the objectives of the assignment.

Although observation can provide some insight on group effectiveness and individual performance, it works best when used in conjunction with detailed feedback from the group members themselves. Since the members of the teams are best equipped to assess their teammates' and their own contributions to the project, many teachers now include their students' voices in the final evaluation process. For example, both David Meredith (Engineering) and Larry Spence (Political Science) have reported good results from using a simple point system for evaluating individual contributions to the group. Meredith tells us that he asks each student to "allocate a fixed number of points (say twenty) among the rest of the team members. The values are averaged for each student, and form a weighting factor for the final team project score."

Many teachers elaborate on this idea by asking students to complete peer assessment forms when the project is complete. These forms generally include a point system similar to the one described above, and spaces for confidential comments about the contribution of each group member. Usually, the student is asked to include a self-assessment on the form, so that the teacher may understand how the student perceives his or her own contribution to the group in relation to that of other members. Robert Melton (Aerospace Engineering) requires students to complete a form that asks about the dependability, accuracy, and value of each team member's contribution to the project. In addition, the students assign a numerical rank and qualitative assessment to the contributions of each group member—including themselves. Likewise, Kathryn Dansky (Health Policy and Administration) asks students to assign numerical scores to each team member (including themselves) in five major areas: leadership, cooperation, communication, work ethic, and quality of work.

Finally, these student assessments of group process and individual contribution can be combined with your evaluation of the team's product to determine each student's final project grade. In your calculations you will weight the two scores according to the objectives of the assignment, but in general, peer assessment tends to determine from 5% to 30% of the project grade. In cases where successful group process is as important an objective as is the product, the two scores might be weighted equally. Whichever method you choose, inform the students of the grading policy at the start of the project, so that your expectations for the assignment are clear. Grading collaborative activities is always challenging, but with peer assessment, individual performance can be rewarded while each student's grade still depends largely on the success of the entire group.

In what ways can technology support the goals of collaborative learning? —Just as technology can serve the lecture and discussion methods of teaching, it can also be used as a tool to address some of the challenges presented by collaborative activities. Many of the uses of technology for group projects work well in any discipline, and are simple to plan and implement. For example, assigning periodic group progress reports to be submitted by e-mail is an easy way to keep up with each group's project, and your e-mail response can be sent to each team member. E-mail also simplifies out-of-class communication within the groups, since students often use it to exchange ideas and set up meetings. This idea is taken a step farther in the English department, where students writing collaboratively provide feedback on each other's writing using Common Space, a communication and feedback software. Because the students' comments appear in separate columns set up for each writer, this software facilitates collaborative writing by bringing together feedback from each group member onto one draft, without losing track of the source of each response. In addition, the software converts documents from different word processing programs and operating systems, allowing drafts and feedback to be sent quickly and easily to group members as e-mail attachments. The use of e-mail progress reports and collaborative writing software also prepares graduates for their entry to the workplace, where such tools are increasingly being used to support collaboration and communication. Other teachers have used technology by creating World Wide Web sites that serve as resources for students working on collaborative projects. One excellent example of this idea is the Engineering Design and Graphics 100 Web site, 7 created and maintained by Dhushy Sathianathan (Engineering Design and

Graphics). This award-winning site combines resources for the course's collaborative design assignments, space for the student Web sites which are a requirement of each group project, and links to the Web sites of all the teachers of ED&G 100. As resources for design projects, Sathianathan has included an outline of the engineering design process, guidelines for the reports students will complete, and several project management and assessment tools. These tools, along with the class itself, help students identify and develop the skills needed to form an effective team. The site supports students as they learn to plan and run a productive meeting, use action plans and progress reports, and perform self-assessment to track the progress of the team. Such management tools help to address many of the challenges of collaboration, such as learning to work in groups and communicating in ways that defuse potential group conflicts. Sathianathan's site also includes assessment and evaluation forms that students use to evaluate the contributions made by their teammates and themselves. Past and present student projects make the site as dynamic as it is helpful.

The ED&G 100 site clearly shows the critical role of students in the collaborative classroom. Indeed, with or without the tools of technology, the true strength of collaborative methods is that they allow students to work together to build their individual skills. When students learn through discussion and exploration, they establish ownership of the material.

Activity Three: Discussion and practice

With the theory and knowledge about collaborative learning, design one activity for the students to accomplish in groups.

Voice from the Theory

COLLABORATIVE LEARNING

Various names have been given to this form of teaching, and there are some distinctions among these: cooperative learning, collaborative learning, collective learning, learning communities, peer teaching, peer learning, reciprocal learning, team learning, study circles, study groups, and work groups. But all in all, there are three general types of group work: informal learning groups, formal learning groups, and study teams (adapted from Johnson, Johnson, and Smith, 1991).

INFORMAL LEARNING GROUPS

Informal learning groups are ad hoc temporary clusterings of students within a single class session. Informal learning groups can be initiated, for example, by asking students to turn to a neighbor and spend two minutes discussing a question you have posed. You can also form groups of three to five to solve a problem or pose a question. You can organize informal groups at any time in a class of any size to check on students' understanding of the material, to give students an opportunity to apply what they are learning, or to provide a change of pace.

FORMAL LEARNING GROUPS

Formal learning groups are teams established to complete a specific task, such as perform a lab experiment, write a report, carry out a project, or prepare a position paper. These groups may complete their work in a single class session or over several weeks. Typically, students work together until the task is finished, and their project is graded.

STUDY TEAMS

Study teams are long-term groups (usually existing over the course of a semester) with stable membership whose primary responsibility is to provide members with support, encouragement, and assistance in completing course requirements and assignments. Study teams also inform their members about lectures and assignments when someone has missed a session. The larger the class and the more complex the subject matter, the more valuable study teams can be.

Bibliography

Beckman, M. 1990. Collaborative Learning: Preparation for the Workplace and Democracy [J]. *College Teaching*. 38(4), 128-133.

Johnson, D. W., Johnson, R. T., and Smith, K. A. 1991. *Cooperative Learning: Increasing College Faculty Instructional Productivity* [R]. ASHE - FRIC Higher Education Report No. 4.

Washington, D. C.: School of Education and Human Development, George Washington University.

Slavin, R. F. 1980. Cooperative Learning[J]. *Review of Educational Research*. 1980, 50(2), 315-342.

Slavin, R. E. 1983. When Does Cooperative Learning Increase Student Achievement? [J]. *Psychological Bulletin*. 94(3), 429-445.

Smith, K. A. 1986. Cooperative Learning Groups[C]. In S. F. Schmoberg (ed.), Strategies for Active Teaching and Learning in University Classrooms. Minneapolis: Office of Educational Development Programs, University of Minnesota.

Whitman, N. A. 1988. *Peer Teaching: To Teach Is to Learn Twice* [C]. Washington, D. C.: ASHE-ERIC Higher Education Report No. 4. Washington, D. C.: Association for the Study of Higher Education.

Module Eight

Logistics English Teachers' Professional Development

Discussion:

◇ How do you understand the changes of terms for English teachers' professional development?

◇ What are the strategies for Professional Development (PD)?

◇ What are the professional development of logistics English teachers?

Section 1 Understanding Professional Development

Problem and Reflection

Activity One: Lead-in knowledge

The following terms are used to refer to teachers' development in pedagogy. The change of use in history is as follows. Explore the difference of these terms and guess the reasons of changing.

Teacher training —— teacher education —— teacher development/teacher preparation/professional development

Activity Two: Reading

1. Read the following article named "Development for survival and progress" written by Ur. (2000:318)

A teacher can and should advance in professional expertise and knowledge throughout his or her career, and such advances do not depend on formal courses or external input. You have within your own teaching routine the main tools for personal progress: your own experience and reflections on it, interaction with other teachers in your instruction. Teacher development takes place when teachers, working as individuals or in a group, consciously take advantage of such resources to forward their own professional learning.

Ongoing teacher development is important not only for your own sense of progress and professional advancement, in some situations it may even make a crucial difference between survival and dropping out.

The first year of teaching, for example, can be very stressful. This is true particularly, though not only, of those teaching large heterogeneous classes of children or adolescents in schools. Difficult first years cause some new teachers to leave the profession, and even many of those who remain find their original confidence and optimism significantly, if temporarily, undermined.

There is also a problem of professional survival in later years of one's career, caused by the phenomenon known as "burn-out". This is not so much a feeling of failure as one of disillusionment, boredom, loss of momentum. Burn-out usually comes on gradually, although it may be accelerated by personal crises such as family or financial problems. Sometimes burn-out may be ended only by retirement or a change of profession, but it may also be prevented or cured by deliberate action on the part of the teacher.

Constant teacher development and progress can forestall or solve problems caused by both first-year stress and later burn-out. More positively, it is a necessary contributor to your success and satisfaction in professional work today, and to your career in the future as teacher and/or in other allied professions: materials writer, trainer, author, researcher.

Post-reading task:

Do you find the answer of activity one from the reading? Combined your own experiences as a logistics English teacher, give the detailed explanation to that.

2. Now read an article written by a Chinese teacher about China's condition. (Transcribed from a speech at the 1st International Annual Conference of TEFL-CHINA,2002)

The professionalization of teaching has had undergone a long process in China's history. The training of teachers started in 1681when the first Normal School was set up by the early Christian missionaries. But the concept of professionalization of teaching was not put forward until the 1980s, when we no longer face the problem of an inadequate number of teachers. Since then sociologists and educators have had explored the concept of teaching as a profession, and agreed that teachers are professionals next to doctors and lawyers. There also arose a general notion that a profession is not equivalent to a trade.

- Firstly, it has an indispensable social function,
- Secondly, it has developed consistent theories and necessary skills,
- Thirdly, the profession has its own autonomous and authoritative organization.

If the teaching of foreign language is a profession, then it has to possess these qualifications.

How can teachers of English as a Foreign Language develop their competency to become true professionals?

This is a question that we need to ponder seriously when the Chinese government and the society at large set an unprecedented high demand on the teaching of foreign languages.

The models of teacher education programs in the past are generally based on nine-skills:

Knowledge of content of teaching and skills of teaching. This chapter attempts to show that this model is no longer applicable in the new era and that our profession is multidisciplinary and full of variables. The expertise of EFL teacher also might be compared to cognitive proficiency and specific techniques in the awareness of the working system of the profession and awareness of the multifaceted nature of language and the multidisciplinary nature of language teaching. The development of such kind of awareness and the ability to handle the competitiveness of language teaching and learning should be incorporated in the objectives of teacher education in the new century.

Activity Three: Discussion

How can the logistics English teachers in China develop their competency to become true professionals? Support the idea with the evidence from your daily teaching.

Voice from the Theory

TEACHER DEVELOPMENT

Teacher DeveLopment (TD) is very broad in scope, and potentially takes in many aspects of a teacher's personal development alongside more mainstream professional areas. The term is frequently contrasted with "teacher training" and "teacher education". Wallace (1991: 3) puts it straight-forwardly: "The distinction is that training or education is something that can be presented or managed by *others*; whereas development is something that can be done only by and for *oneself*."

Section 2 Strategies for Logistics English Teachers' Professional Development

Problem and Reflection

Activity One:

1. Tick 3 of the possible ways you have ever used for professional development as a logistics English teacher.

- Reading academic journals/books
- Conferences/lectures
- Accessing Internet resources
- Discussion with others (talking shop)
- Self-reflection
- Colleagues' feedback based on classroom observation
- Students' feedback
- Classroom research
- Staff training development session
- Material writing
- In-service courses in some companies

2. If you have other ways for PD of the logistics teachers, list them here, and then compare them with other teachers.

____

____

____

Activity Two: Reading

Read the article "A literature review of teacher development" (Gilbert, 1993). Think of the present conditions of Chinese logistics English teaching and your tasks as a logistics English teacher.

Teachers themselves are concerned about change and about their own personal and professional development. Every year large numbers of teachers participate in in-service programmes in a variety of forms. This participation is usually the result of their own personal initiative, representing a commitment to the enhancement of their own professional development (Education Review Office, 1990; Wylie, 1992: 128). Teachers as a group are concerned with the nature of their practice and continually seek new and innovative ways to enhance student learning. These teachers return to their classrooms after attending professional development programmes, believing themselves ready to use new techniques, new curriculum materials or new content knowledge in new ways that will improve the learning of their students. Unfortunately, it is common for teachers to find themselves teaching in the same way they always have, perhaps utilising some of the new materials but adapting them to fit traditional patterns (Briscoe, 1991). Many teachers are aware of this pattern and feel frustrated in their attempts to change.

In addition to the personal frustrations felt by teachers in their attempts to improve their practice, the work of curriculum developers and researchers has begun to acknowledge the powerful influence teachers have on the curriculum implementation process (Cronin-Jones, 1991). Research has indicated that teachers do not necessarily implement curriculum initiatives in their classes in the way that these curricula were designed to be implemented (Doyle and Ponder, 1977; Roberts, 1982; Smith and Anderson, 1984), and in science education in particular, researchers have found that even exemplary science teachers have not managed to understand and implement constructivist teaching practices (Tobin, 1990; Tobin and Fraser, 1990; Tobin, Kahle and Fraser, 1990).

Teacher perceptions and beliefs play a critical role in the curriculum implementation process. Each teacher has their own subjective view of the practice of teaching, and teachers are not generally receptive to the implementation of new curricula (Fullan, 1982). When teachers' perceptions are not taken into account in the process of curriculum implementation, their perceptions usually function to hinder the effectiveness of curriculum reform. Tobin (1990:34) argued that previous reforms in science education, which have called for a change in the role of the teacher, have failed because they neglected to take account of essential components in the change process in teacher education. These components were personal reflection on epistemologies and beliefs, the construction of personal visions of classroom practice, and a commitment to personal change.

Therefore, changes in teachers' classroom actions are more likely to occur if the teachers' existing ideas and beliefs are taken into account and developed, as well as the notion of teachers' metacognitive awareness of their own learning. Hence, the teacher development programmes run as part of this research were planned to facilitate not only a change in the teachers' classroom behaviors but also their ideas and beliefs about teaching and learning, the nature of science and the science curriculum. Previous research on the factors which facilitate changes in teacher behavior indicated that it is important that teacher professional development programmes provide opportunities for teachers to develop their implicit theories of learning and to reflect on their personal concerns and problems with teaching, on their actions in the classroom, on the implications of their implicit theories of learning for their ability to provide opportunities for conceptual change for their students, and on the process of change (Fullan,1982).

Previous research has also indicated that this articulation, clarification and reflection by teachers on their personal theories about learning is best done in an environment in which they can collaborate with, and receive support from other teachers who work in similar situations, and that this should be done in an ongoing and interactive way, allowing sufficient time and space for it to happen (Fullan, 1988).

Also, if teacher professional development is to result in teachers who can do something more than just re – create the teaching practices that they themselves experienced (Grumet, 1980), we need a means of enabling teachers to learn—in the constructivist sense—about their own learning. We need a means through which teachers can be enabled to develop an awareness of, and be able to articulate their prior knowledge and beliefs, an awareness of the importance of the context in which their learning takes place. In much of the current literature on teacher development, it is argued that teachers must engage in the kinds of critical reflection that permits them to reclaim and surpass their own histories (Grumet, 1980).

Activity Three: Discussion

This book presents training activities to some of the logistics English teachers' competences. As a logistics English teacher, what other competences need to be equipped? List them and state the reasons.

Bibliography

Gilbert, J. 1993 Teacher Development: A Literature Review[C]. In B. Bell(ed) *I know about LISP but how do I put it into practice*? Hamilton: Center for Science and Mathematics Education Research.

Johnson, K., Johnson, H. 1999. *Encyclopedic Dictionary of Applied Linguistics: A Handbook for Language Teaching* [M]. Blackwell Publishers Ltd.

Wallace, M. J. 1992. *Training Foreign Language Teachers* [M]. Cambridge: Cambridge University Press.

Appendix：

访谈实录

1.

时间:2012年7月2日

地点:舟山市港航局会议室

访谈要点摘录:

舟山港域位于太平洋西部,远东航运网络中心地带,地处我国长江三角洲和东部沿海要冲,是长三角综合运输网的重要节点,是国际物流和国内物流的结合区域。

Interviewee：2011年6月30日,国务院正式批复设立浙江舟山群岛新区,舟山建设上升为国家发展战略。舟山群岛新区成为浙江海洋经济发展的先导区、海洋综合开发试验区和长江三角洲地区经济发展的重要增长极,逐步建成我国大宗商品储运中转加工交易中心、东部地区重要的海上开放门户、海洋海岛综合保护开发示范区、重要的现代海洋产业基地、陆海统筹发展先行区,在推动浙江经济社会发展、推进东部地区发展方式转变、促进全国区域协调发展中发挥更大作用。

Interviewer：新区作为国际物流岛的定位及主要优势体现在哪些方面?

Interviewee：国务院批准的《浙江海洋经济发展示范区规划》赋予舟山海洋经济先行先试的任务,浙江省委省政府构筑"三位一体"港航物流体系战略,将促进舟山港航科学发展、跨越发展、创新发展。舟山市委市政府高度重视港口开发,明确提出"以港兴市、全面跨越"的新目标,举全市之力建设中国(舟山)大宗商品交易中心,抓紧推进舟山保税港区的建设,大力打造国际物流岛,形成亚太地区大宗商品重要的国际枢纽港和国家战略物资储备基地、大宗商品物流基地及交易基地,推进舟山港航新一轮发展。

Interviewer：舟山港在物流方面的主要项目是什么?

Interviewee：舟山港正围绕核心港区,着力建设集装箱、矿砂、煤炭、石油、粮油、化工品六大物流基地,一大批项目正在热火朝天建设之中。随着诸多大型企业的进驻,在这些项目建设投产后,将新增万吨级以上泊位约30个,可为舟山港域新增年吞吐量2亿吨和250万TEU。以港促运,港航联动,推动航运业迅速崛起。

Interviewer:在港口建设的发展过程中,对一些人才的应用有没有什么特殊需求。比如对港口服务人员的外语要求有什么,或者是在港航建设中的外语专业人员的能力有什么具体的规划要求吗?

Interviewee:从港口角度来讲,对外语人才的需求体现在对各种术语的熟练掌握,港口属于一个交叉行业,除了物流、航运,对金融、外汇,包括保险,以及一些新兴的与物流有关系的服务。另一方面在港口发展过程中也需要引进境外的一些银行、金融单位、保险等。对外语人才的要求不仅仅是英语能力,对港口、物流以及其他相关配套服务能够更精通。

Interviewee:外语专业人才进入港航局工作以后,为适应新的岗位要求,可能采取的或者是希望采取的培训学习方式是什么?

Interviewee B:在当前港航局的工作条件下,更希望在工作中通过实践模式进行再学习。更多地体现在专业术语上的不断习得与不断强化使用。

Interviewee:针对物流方面的学习,你更愿意选择哪种,是学历性学习还是短期的实用性学习。

Interviewee B:我个人很愿意系统地学习一些物流专业知识,但是单位的条件不允许。所以在职学习也是一种有效的途径。我个人目前实施的就是这种模式。从实践中来,到实践中去。学习的效果可以及时地得到验证与补充。

2.

时间:2012年7月29日

地点:鄂尔多斯市金地矿业集团会议室

访谈要点摘录:

天津金地矿业集团公司是国内近年快速发展的一家以煤炭设备改造、煤炭深加工、煤炭销售与煤炭运输为一体的大型民营企业。作为当前国内经济社会中具有重要影响力的煤炭行业集团,几个子公司分处内蒙古鄂尔多斯市、北京市、天津市,分别担负着运营、设计与贸易物流几大功能。

Interviewer:天津金地矿业集团公司作为国内大型的煤炭行业集团,其业务功能涉及煤炭相关的许多领域。在煤炭设计、运营与销售过程中,物流运输承担着重要作用。那么公司在物流方面的主要理念是什么?

Interviewee:物流是服务于经营与销售的一个重要环节,在公司的对外物流操作中,一个核心理念就是环保。过去我们曾经与中铁物流联合,在内蒙古包头引用澳大利亚的先进技术与管理手段,实现万吨列车45分钟装车。占用土地少,而且通过行走时装车,实现了污染少、效率高、费用相对降低的预期目标。

Interviewer:鄂尔多斯市近年在全国经济中因其突出的各项指标备受关注,而煤炭行业又是关注中的焦点。随着市场的几起几落,行业竞争中最重要的因素体现在哪里?

Interviewee:竞争中的利刃是市场、资金与人才。尽管现在经济危机的影响已经可以感觉到了,但我们公司依托先进的技术,将落后式开采转为自动化程度很高的运营操作,通过港口直接销售,竞争中还是体现了突出的优势。因此,市场占有率较高,发展前景较好。产品有市场,资金的调配也就非常顺畅。现在公司主要欠缺的就是“人才”。得“天下英才而兴业”是我们的目标。

Interviewer:现在企业的人才培养模式是什么?

Interviewee:主要是两种途径:自己培养与引进。集团公司刚刚在美国注册一家公司,同时在国内注册成立“美森工业技术有限公司”,实现组装、研发与物流中心三大版块的协作发展。通过美国的信息平台与国内呼应,引进、消化、自主开发作为主要链条模式,实现产品的尽快转化与产业化。在整个研发与改造过程中,我们计划自主培养一批既能适应国内经济运行模式,生产战斗力强,又能融合国外最新研究成果,并能迅速投入到生产实践中的人员。在培养过程中,专业人员的外语应用能力需要强化并专业化。而外语人才的专业能力不仅体现在煤炭技术,也体现在运营、销售与国际物流等领域。同时我们还计划引进一批优秀人才。在企业支撑下,实现产品研发、试验与应用一体化。

后　记

物流英语的研究兴趣源于北京物资学院，一个充满了物流氛围的校园。“人尽其才，地尽其利，物尽其用，货畅其流”是孙中山先生早年的倡导。今天，在物流学理论，特别是物流实践的飞速发展中，我们正在努力实现先生的心愿。

由于资本与产品的全球性流动，物流国际化发展成为一种必需。经济的发展自发地要求所有产业都要与物流业结合。随着国际物流的发展，物流英语不可替代地产生了。一些最新的国际物流术语迅速传播，物流操作的实用性也强化了物流英语语言表达的便捷性。现代物流英语紧贴物流学科的最新发展趋势，反映前沿的现代物流理论及物流管理各环节的基本概念与业务知识。实践的发展与理论水平的提高相辅相成，在国际物流运行与操作中，物流英语作为物流行业的规范英语，它服务于物流产业，执行国际物流操作，提高国际物流运作的效率，推进了国际物流的专业化发展。它的行业服务作用正在引起物流领域及外语教育领域人士的关注。

本书从物流行业入手，不仅关注行业发展，更关心行业发展背后的“源”。“问渠那得清如许，为有源头活水来”。只有从物流行业人才的培养着眼，才能保证物流业发展的可持续供应。

本书仅仅选取了物流英语这样一个小小的研究角落，从物流英语教师的专业化发展开始讨论，引导行业人员关注自身发展，以自己为资源，带动行业群体的综合发展。

本书的所有活动都是基于理论思考与实践的同步要求。对企业物流实践的访谈也是保证训练项目满足企业直接需求。“从实践中来，到实践中去”，更希望我们的训练项目能得到更多企业的实践检验。

本书的许多素材来自北京物资学院的物流英语教学实践，并且得到了学校领导老师的诸多无私帮助，在此表示深深的感谢！

我们认认真真地对待，却依然存在很多问题，还请尊敬的读者批评指正。